December 2011

To an "old
Coonhaunter —
Many more good!
times to come!
Love —
Le Ann

Emma

The Autobiography of a
Treeing Walker Coonhound

Linda Gannon

iUniverse, Inc.
Bloomington

The Autobiography of a Treeing Walker Coonhound
Emma

iUniverse books may be ordered through booksellers or by contacting:

iUniverse
1663 Liberty Drive
Bloomington, IN 47403
www.iuniverse.com
1-800-Authors (1-800-288-4677)

ISBN: 978-1-4502-8000-6 (pbk)
ISBN: 978-1-4502-8001-3 (cloth)
ISBN: 978-1-4502-8002-0 (ebk)

Printed in the United States of America

iUniverse rev. date: 1/13/11

Dedication

To George Moskos, 1948-2011.

Table of Contents

List of Illustrations

Acknowledgments

Thanks to Lynne Hofling for the cover design and layout; to George Moskos for editing assistance; and to my friends and family who have accepted and appreciated me for who I am, someone who more easily befriends animals than people.

The poem in the Epilogue is from Twelve Moons by Mary Oliver. Copyright 1972, 1973, 1974, 1976, 1977, 1977, 1978, 1979 by Mary Oliver. By permission of Little. Brown, and Company.

A Star is Born

I was born on a bright, sunny morning in Murphysboro, Illinois on April 4, 1990. I was the third of eight. I can't say I was pleased to emerge from a warm, dark nourishing place to a world of noise and legs—lots of legs. After much confusion and scrambling about, I found a comforting spot and some nourishment. Unfortunately, there was only room for 6 at meal time. This screw-up of nature gave me my first lesson—grab what food you can before you get pushed out of the way. In spite of this early nutritional deprivation, all eight of us were bigger, smarter and healthier than most coonhound pups. We descended from royalty—both ma and pa were national champions for doing whatever it is we are supposed to do as adults. I was never clear on the details of the coonhound profession—my life developed in a direction different from that of most coonhounds.

Early on, ma realized that eight puppies required "proactive" adoption strategies. She needed eight wonderful homes, and she wasn't going to let humans decide the fate of her pups. If she had anything to do with the decisions, and she planned to do just that, these little budding princes and princesses were going to homes where they would be appreciated, loved, and given the opportunity to "show their stuff." Often she wandered around the yard early in the morning to escape the drudgery of motherhood—eight hungry, squabbling brats were wearing her down, especially after we got teeth. One morning, she noticed a woman jogging along the road. Our yard was apparently on the woman's jogging route because ma noticed the same woman day after day. When ma went down to the road to investigate, the woman stopped to have a chat and pet her. Always on the look-out for prospective adoptive parents, ma tried to make a good impression—she pretended to be "sweet" and tried to act "adorable." These are not the traits for which coonhounds are known but Ma was a good actress.

After a few weeks of pets and chats, ma decided to accept this woman as an applicant for adoption so she rolled on her back to expose her full nipples, assuming the woman would make the connection that nipples meant puppies and that puppies meant potential adoption opportunities. Well, this woman was a bit dense. Ma had to roll over three mornings in a row before the jogging woman "got it." And just in time. Ma had begun to question if the woman was bright enough to be a proper companion to a coonhound. Finally, this woman asked ma's human if she could see the puppies (good first step). Well, right away you could tell here was a real sap for "cute" and we were all cute (I was the cutest). She forgot all about her jogging; she played and petted and cuddled and kissed the tops of heads. She asked if the puppies were available for adoption (good second step). But then she blew it.

The woman asked what kind of dog my father was. Well!!!!!!!. Here ma's human went to all the trouble of training her pure bred Treeing Walker Coonhound to be a champion and traveling all over the country to show her stuff and, finally, to find a boy Treeing Walker Coonhound who was also a champion to be the daddy, and some dumb woman mistook us puppies for "mixed." We were rather conceited from hearing our parents' stories about how they won their championships, so we were all a bit put out. Ma's person patiently and politely explained the royal line of descent. Although delighted at the prospect of one less for meals, ma was having second thoughts about the woman's qualifications as a potential companion—certainly a coonhound companion should understand and appreciate coonhoundship. The jogger seemed to realize she messed up. She apologized and then apologized again. She said she was from Wisconsin where they didn't have coonhounds so she had never seen a real one. Must be a real sad place—Wisconsin. Then one more time, she apologized. She said she thought ma was beautiful and that she really liked the puppies. She promised to give one a good home. She put it all on a bit heavy but, as it turned out, she was convincing. The deal was done. The woman just had to wait till we were old enough. Well, I wondered, "old enough for what?"

"Old enough" turned out to be about the time ma started getting stingy about meals. And here came this jogger back with two men friends who were visiting her from afar—Blair and George. The three of them played with all of us—they examined our spots and our ears and even inspected our bottoms (why?). They even discussed our personalities as if they had a clue as to what a good coonhound personality was or of what feats a coonhound was capable. None of us understood the point of all this but we were having fun trying to eat their buttons and chewing on their shoes. Then one of the men picked me up. He was fascinated by a little, tiny spot on my hip and said wonderful things about my character. He was right on about two traits—"very intelligent" and "a mind of her own;" he was wrong about "gentle" and "laid back."

And then everything happened quickly. Before I knew what was going on, I was being carried to a horrible, hot metal cage (later I learned this was a car). I was placed on the lap of one of the men and away we went. I was being taken further and further away from that nipple I had fought so hard to get; I was being separated from my buddies; I was in a very strange and noisy contraption with humans who smelled funny. I was definitely not happy. I did what any self-respecting coonhound would do when deprived of food and fun. I howled and howled and howled. And one trait (of many) in which coonhounds excel over all other breeds is their loud wonderful piercing voice. At first this frightened the humans. The machine stopped moving and they all stared at me. But as soon as they realized I wasn't hurt or sick, just expressing my displeasure, they started moving again. They did not take me back home.

Finally, and I do mean finally, I got out of that horrible machine. I didn't know where I was or what to do. No nipples, no brothers, no sisters, no ma. I got depressed and moped and moped and moped. The woman realized I was unhappy, and she picked me up, petted me, and carried me around with her—I must admit that felt good. Actually, she was beginning to smell good to me. She gave me a "teddy bear." It was about my size. I could bite it and chew on it just like I had my brothers and sisters—in fact, we named it "Sibling." At night, when it was quiet and people slept, I felt lonely for my brothers and sisters and missed cuddling up to ma at night. The woman had given me a little bed on the floor near where she slept, and I had Sibling for company, but it wasn't enough. I wasn't happy. So the woman started taking me to bed with her. She even let me bring Sibling along. Somehow I managed to sandwich myself between the woman and Sibling so I could touch both of them and was finally able to get a good night's sleep. This woman may not have known a coonhound when she saw one but she knew how to make a coonhound puppy happy.

This seemed to be where I was going to live so I thought it was time I used my great powers of observation and keen intelligence to make a good life here. So I watched, listened, attended, and tried to figure it all out. This was not really a bad place. My new home was in the middle of a vast woods filled with all sorts of wild life, including, of course, my specialty, raccoons, with a lake near the house. There were no other houses near by, no cars, no roads. Very quiet and peaceful. There were no nipples but there was good food. Unfortunately, I had to chew the food rather than just inhale it but it tasted good, and I got as much as I wanted. I didn't have to fight off the other pups. I figured out early on that this woman, who seemed in charge of the place, wasn't truly stupid and could, without much effort on my part, be manipulated into just about anything. If I showed an interest in her food, she gave me some. This, however, was something of a disappointment. I was adopted by a vegetarian. Can you imagine a coonhound, whose favorite food is fresh road-kill, adopted by a vegetarian? At least she ate cheese, which she shared, and, thankfully, she didn't expect me to be a vegetarian.

For several weeks after arriving at this place, one big problem was names. What was my name, what was her name? Initially, the woman called me Phoebe. A champion coonhound named Phoebe? I don't think so—a bit too cute and sweet. To get a more appropriate name was easy. I just ignored anyone who called me "Phoebe." Other names were tried. Blair and George were still visiting, and three humans generated many, many names. I didn't like any of them so I just ignored their efforts. But then someone hit on "Emma." There was something about "Emma" that appealed to me. It was simple, strong, not too feminine. So "Emma" it was. When I heard that name, I trotted over to whoever said it and looked expectant and cute. They caught on pretty quickly and I became Emma. When I got older, I occasionally heard it said about my name, "well, it is clear she was named after an early 20ᵗʰ century anarchist and feminist and not a genteel, 19ᵗʰ century literary heroine obsessed with her friends' love lives."

Now I needed names for them. But, as it turned out, awhile after I arrived, the two men left. The woman and I were alone, and this seemed to be the "permanent" state of affairs. Obviously, I had to come up with a name for her. This took some careful thought. She obviously thought she was "in charge." Of course, no human could be "in charge" of a coonhound but she, obviously, needed to believe that she was the boss. My name for her needed to reflect my false acknowledgment of her false authority. But the meaning of the name had to be ambiguous to her. I didn't want her to underestimate me but she would be easier to manipulate if she occasionally felt complacent. If she told me to do something and I didn't do it, I wanted her to question if it was my IQ, my hearing, my independence, or a stupid request. On the other hand, there was no way I was actually going to defer to anyone or anything so the name had to convey a sense of sarcasm but sarcasm that wouldn't be too obvious to her. I needed a name that conveyed both obsequiousness and mockery. I finally settled on "My Own Perfect Potentate" which quickly turned to MOPP. So I was Emma and she was Mopp. Mopp thought my name for her was humorous. Then I worried that I had underestimated her. Perhaps she understood me too well.

I was getting used to my new home—my permanent home. I had a special place for my food and water bowls. I had good, though a bit boring, food. In those first few months, I followed Mopp around while she did various chores in the house and in the great outdoors. I quickly learned that the "hot metal cage" wasn't all bad. Mopp used it to take us places but, until I showed up, she didn't understand a car's true potential. At first she expected me to sit quietly in the back seat but that was rather boring. So I had to make it clear to her that my place was in the front with the seat pushed back as far as possible with the window open all the way so that I could get my head and neck out the window. There were great smells out there and I didn't want to miss a one of them. Mopp learned that part quickly but she did insist that I not sit on her lap and stick my head out her window. She wouldn't relent on that one. She also learned not to complain about drool on the windows and the dashboard—what does she expect??? I smell something good and drool—that's perfectly natural. Does she expect a coonhound to carry tissues???? But she did complain (loudly) that the open window let in cold air in the winter and hot air in the summer. I agreed that that was a problem but there was an easy solution—just turn on the heat or the air conditioning. That seemed to me to be the only way to go. I could have my head out the window and smell each and every thing we passed while my body was being "temperature controlled." Great. She finally, but slowly, learned this important lesson but often grumbled saying "I can't believe I'm doing this." Well, it was hard to believe how long it took her to catch on—not terribly bright. She was lucky she had me.

Sometimes we used the car to visit friends. Shortly after I came to live with Mopp, we went to visit her friend Kelly. And Kelly had a dog companion named Hawken. Hawken became my very best friend in the whole world. He was sort of a golden lab and about a year older than me. The first time I met him, he took me outside his house to show me his yard and what he called a great prize. We went behind his house, and he started digging. Well, this was interesting. I never thought to use my feet like that. But there, under a bunch of dirt, was a great smelling, nicely aged bone with a little meat still on it. He wouldn't let me have the bone. He just put it back in the hole,

7

and covered it up again. I was impressed. His house had bones in the dirt. I wondered if my house had dirt with bones in it. Eventually, Hawken taught me that he had buried the bone so that no one else could get it and he would be able to find it when he was hungry. This was certainly useful information but I never made much use of it because I had a little problem with delayed gratification—if there was a bone, I wanted it now. I wasn't good at "saving" for a rainy day. But I did use this information to dig up prizes that other dogs had buried.

As we left Hawken's house that day, Mopp said that Kelly was a wonderful friend but that I had to be very very careful with people I didn't know because I was so smart and so beautiful (I knew that)—someone might want to take me home with them. When I was a pup, that made no impression on me. I thought, "What's so bad about that? Maybe they have more food at their house, maybe they aren't vegetarians and cook more interesting stuff." But, as I met other dogs, I learned that some dogs didn't have a couch, some weren't allowed indoors, some weren't allowed outdoors, and some even lived in a cage or were tied to a rope. I planned to be very very careful of strangers.

School

After a few weeks in my new home, Mopp announced that there were a few things I needed to learn. If Mopp were writing this, she would label this "training." Initially, she made the mistake of thinking of me as any old dog—a dog who would take orders, behave according to human rules, obey. But I am not a lab or a poodle but a coonhound and coonhounds have a purpose that is not to be constrained or limited by humans. My purpose was to track raccoons with as much noise and vigor as possible, and to do this, I needed freedom, comfort, good food, and, above, all respect and appreciation. On the other hand, Mopp had to be appeased since I needed her to supply the necessary goodies. So we negotiated.

The first "issue" was peeing and pooping. Since I had been raised properly, I never peed or pooped in places where I wanted to sleep or near my food. But I had thought that the rest of the world was fair game. Mopp, however, had different ideas. At first I thought I wasn't supposed to go where she ate or slept. So I didn't use the kitchen or the bed but Mopp made it quite clear that there were other "inappropriate" areas. Whenever Mopp saw me about to do "it," she swooped me up and took me outside and, importantly, gave me a biscuit if I "went." I learned quickly when food was the reward. I finally got it—"outside" was OK, "inside" was not OK. The porch was a point of contention for awhile—she said the porch was "inside," I said "outside." Biscuits finally converted me to her way of thinking. Why didn't she have to "go" outside?

So the first negotiation was relatively easy. Fine. But how do I get outside when I am inside? Mopp wasn't always there to open the door—what was I supposed to do???? Getting outside wasn't a problem at night. Because I slept next to or on top of Mopp, she woke up if I squirmed around. Then she carried me outside, let me pee, gave me a biscuit, carried me back inside, and took me back to bed with her (was I spoiled or what?). But days were another story. She explained that she had to leave sometimes so that she could earn money so she could buy stuff for me. I fully agreed that she needed to buy stuff for me. BUT I explained that having to wait when you have to "go" places unnecessary physical and psychological stress on a growing coonhound. Mopp is such a push-over. Guess what I got!!!!! A doggy door. This was my idea of heaven. If I didn't like the weather outside, I came in and slept on the bed or got a snack. If I had to "go" or if a wanted a little sun or a little air, I went out and snoozed on the deck. If there was a disturbance in the woods, I was out like a shot to do whatever needed to be done. Forty acres of forest and a lake to patrol was hard work. But when I was satisfied that everything was under control, I had access to a temperature-controlled environment and a comfortable bed. Perfect solution. Mopp seemed to think so too. We were both very content for awhile.

School—oh my goddess, have you ever heard of a coonhound going to school? I knew all I needed to know—I didn't need school. I think I was about 6 months old and Mopp must have been senile to think this one up. It began OK. Mopp got treats out of the frig and put them in a bag and brought them along in the car. A good sign, we weren't leaving home without food. Finally, after a long drive, we arrived at this place with lots of grass, trees, and big buildings. Mopp put me on a leash (a leash is always a bad sign because it means that she and I would want to go in different directions). We walked into a large room in a huge building. I took one look at 20 humans standing next to 20 dogs—not one coonhound in the bunch. German Shephards, labs, poodles—poodles??? Give me a break. I pulled out of my collar and left. The door was closed and I couldn't get out. Mopp was advancing on me. I couldn't escape so I did the next best thing—I peed. Mopp wasn't as mad as I expected. She just put my collar back on, picked me up (I wasn't at my full weight yet) and carried me into this room with poodles.

Then I remembered the treats she had brought. Well, maybe I could do a little of this. So I "sat," I "stayed," but I refused, absolutely refused, to "lie down" and usually refused to "heel." Sometimes the "heel" command told me to go in the same direction I was planning to go anyway so I appeared to sort of learn this one. Luckily, "sit" and "stay" were always first so I managed to get all the treats before we got to "heel" and "down." How incredibly, utterly, stupidly boring the whole thing was. I think Mopp found it a bit much also. We went to all six of the classes but we never stayed until the end of any class. She always blamed our leaving early on me. She told the teacher that I had a short attention span so that we had to leave a little early. She's got to be kidding. I can attend to a raccoon for 20 hours if need be. I think she had a short attention span. So I learned the words "sit" and "stay" and obeyed when I felt like it—there has usually been no need to do either.

The next "lesson" involved food. I had a rather extraordinary appetite. I loved just about any food except vegetables and fruit although I occasionally was willing to eat a carrot just to make Mopp happy. My normal food was OK but not great. After all, it came out of a bag. Real food, good food is in the woods—running around. As I mentioned earlier, my strengths were tracking and treeing. I was rather weak on catching and killing my own food. In an abstract way, I understood that to catch a meal, I had to sneak up on the critter very, very quietly. No one is going to sit around waiting to be my dinner. But as soon as I smelled something tantalizing, I started howling my head off—I just couldn't help it—it was part of my nature. So to supplement the bagged, boring diet, I spent a bit of time in the woods looking around for stuff that was already dead. The best time, as you might imagine, was hunting season. Mopp hated hunters and wouldn't let them on our land but the hunters were close enough to leave great treats within easy reach.

When I was maybe 8 or 9 months old, I was wandering around one day while Mopp was at work—sniffing this, sniffing that and suddenly detected a great, great prize. I followed my nose, as they say, and found this wonderful dead deer. Well, it wasn't newly dead and had been picked over a bit already. But I found a good bone (rather large actually—Mopp later referred to it as the "spinal cord" whatever that is) and took it home, through the doggy door—which was not easy—hopped up on Mopp's bed and started to enjoy a really good chew. Mopp came home. I expected her to be rather proud of me for having found this prize. I was careful not to appear to enjoy it too much—I certainly didn't want Mopp to think I could find my own food and stop giving me the bagged stuff. But she was mad. I never did understand her species. She threw my spinal cord into the lake—into the lake???? I hate to swim. She then talked to herself while she washed the sheets and blankets that had been on the bed.

This little scene repeated itself. I'd go back to the dead deer, get a little tidbit, bring it back to Mopp's bed (the best place for a good chew), Mopp would come home and throw it away. I was a little slow to solve this problem because I didn't understand why there was a problem, but problem there was. Eventually I learned to stay outside with whatever little tidbit I had found in the woods. The grass was not as comfortable as Mopp's bed for lying down and chewing but it seemed I didn't have a choice. Actually, some of my prizes were a bit difficult to get through the doggy door so having a picnic was practical. My best friend, Hawken, liked to swim and, when he was around, I considered asking him to get a bit of deer out of the lake after Mopp threw it but he would probably have wanted a percentage. Even if I stayed outside with my goodies, Mopp wasn't wild about my chewing on this stuff. But I'm faster than she is and if she approached me outside while I was chewing, I just picked up the treat and moved out of her reach.

That lesson—permitted goodies inside, forbidden goodies outside—proved to be incredibly useful. I could steal stuff from the kitchen, dash out the doggy door with it, and was free to go off and eat at my leisure. Because I was unusually tall, I could easily get stuff off the kitchen counter. At first, Mopp tried pushing food all the way to the back of the counter. She learned to do this with items she knew I particularly wanted. I had to improvise. If the food I wanted was on a plate and at the back of the counter, I could just manage to reach far enough so that I could slam the plate edge with my paw. This made the other edge of the plate pop up and the food would fly off the plate toward me. This worked great for sandwiches or muffins but a spaghetti dinner or scrambled eggs made a huge mess when it landed on top of my head and all over the floor. I grabbed what I could and ran out the doggy door. When I returned with a full stomach, and after Mopp had washed up the mess, I performed the "I'm so ashamed of myself" look and all would be forgiven. Then I got dinner.

Ice Cubes

There came a day when Mopp regretted the doggy door. When she left to earn money and buy things for me, I found it amusing to chase her car. She didn't seem to mind this if I chased her only to the end of the driveway but if I chased her all the way to the big road, she got mad, put me in the car, and drove me home. And then I chased her again. I knew she didn't want me to do this but it was just too, too tempting. One day I chased her but she was too far ahead and didn't see me. She kept going. I went up to the big road myself just to see what the big deal was. New smells, nothing terribly exciting. Well, this nice old man was up there and he called to me. I wondered how he knew my name. He gave me some water, which I needed, and petted me a bit but then he tied me up—he actually tied me up. I could not believe anyone would do that to me. He put a bucket of water next to me and left me like that for hours. I thought Mopp would be absolutely furious at him for doing this to me. When she finally came home (you will not believe this) she was mad at me but kept thanking this man. Amazing—how could she thank him for tying me up????

The next day, the doggy door was blocked. I was inside, she left. I was miserable. When Mopp came home, I could tell she was miserable too. She hated to make me stay inside. I knew she made me stay inside because I had gone up to the big road by myself, and she was afraid I would do it again. Chasing her car was just so, so tempting that I couldn't promise that I wouldn't do it. Mopp said I had an "impulse" problem. Well, Mopp's problem was that she thought she could solve my problem "creatively." The next day, I could tell something was "up." She was singing—well, with her voice, I hesitate to call it "singing" but it was what she did when she came up with a scheme of some sort.

When it was time for Mopp to leave the next day, she didn't close up the doggy door, she didn't tell me to "stay"—as if I would. She got into the car, said "bye" and took off. I chased, of course. She got to the end of the driveway, stopped, turned around, and drove back to the house. I chased. I figured she forgot something. But she didn't stop at the house. She turned around and drove away again. I chased. She went to the end of the driveway, I chased, she turned around, I chased. It was a mile round trip and 75 degrees—I was getting tired and hot. And then I figured it out. She was planning to get me so tired, I couldn't chase her. HUH!! Fat chance. She drove, I chased, she turned around, I turned around. We did 26 round trips. I stopped. Mopp thought I stopped because I was tired. No way—coonhounds don't get tired. I stopped because—well, just because. I figured I could chase her the next day, which, of course, I did. Her hope that the 26 mile marathon would stop me from chasing the car flopped. And she thought she was so smart. Nope.

For awhile nothing changed. Sometimes she would try to sneak out when she thought I was sleeping, or she would lock me inside. BUT then one morning she was singing again and talking to herself. Another scheme. Although I wasn't learning what she wanted me to learn, I was learning that her schemes often meant that she thought that she had out-smarted me. Out came the saws, hammers, drills. At first I worried she was going to block up the doggy door forever but, no. She had made a flap for the door that fell open unless it was tied shut. Did she go to all this trouble just to block the doggy door??? The next time she left for work, she closed the flap and tied it shut. I thought, oh well, a boring afternoon—nothing new here. I decided to take a nap. After about 10 minutes, I heard a bang from the direction of the doggy door. When I looked, the flap was up, the door free, and there was this suspicious little puddle of water on the floor under the door. I couldn't figure this out. I knew Mopp hadn't come back, I knew the door had been shut—was I dreaming??? I didn't worry about it for too long—I went outside to have some fun.

This sequence of events repeated everytime Mopp left. She had truly found some way to stop me from chasing the car without forcing me to stay inside all day. She was very smug about it all. As I listened to her self-satisfied conversations with her friends, I finally figured out the trick. She tied the door shut with string that she had frozen into an ice cube—when the ice cube melted, the string fell off and the door opened. I did concede that she won that particular battle but she had access to technology—she could not have done it with just her brains and body and no refrigerator. So she won, but she cheated (as humans often do). Occasionally, her friends visited and mistook the ice cubes with strings as specially designed for the purpose of dunking ice in their drinks. Mopp and I both found humor in that one.

My favorite part of the "ice-cube affair" occurred about a week later. Mopp called her mom in California. I met her mom once—nice, nice lady. She was not a vegetarian and willing to share. Anyway, Mopp was telling her about my chasing the car and the 26-mile marathon. She called me a "stubborn,

stubborn, stubborn brat" who went to "all that trouble just to prove a point" and that she hoped I would "grow out of it" soon. Mopp's mom said, "sounds just like you when you were a child and you didn't grow out of it." I loved that.

The Jogging Bull

When I first came to live with Mopp, she went jogging every morning as soon as she woke up and returned about 45 minutes later. I just slept in—fine with me. As I got a bit older, she started saying that "soon" I would go with her. Well, maybe I would, maybe I wouldn't—I had something to say about this. When I was about 6 months old, "morning" changed. Mopp got up and then got me up. She put on my leash and off we went. I was a bit skeptical. We had to go past the yards of some big, mean, nasty dogs who barked. I didn't like that. And I hate being on a leash. It is so undignified and I couldn't follow my nose when I wished. Everytime a car passed, Mopp made me "sit" at the side of the road. That seemed silly. But, after a few weeks, she took off the leash at times and that was more fun. Since we did this every single morning, I learned to stay away from cars and mean dogs and Mopp used the leash less and less. Once I got accustomed to getting up so early, I enjoyed it. There were snacks along the way—squirrel and rabbit road-kill mostly. They were a bit squished but tasty nevertheless. There were often bags from McDonalds or Hardees with a few fries left inside or even a bit of a sandwich (what kind of person puts mustard, of all things, on a hamburger). Once I found an entire spaghetti dinner. After awhile, I came to be as nutty about this jogging business as Mopp. But there were occasional problems.

When I was still quite young and inexperienced about which materials and objects provided a satisfying chew session, I enjoyed ripping apart rolls of toilet paper. I found better materials as I got older but, for a brief time, this was my choice. Often when Mopp came home from work, she had to spend a bit of time picking up the resulting debris. She usually laughed about it so I knew she didn't really mind. I think she preferred it to my chewing on the furniture. One morning as she dressed to jog, I thought I'd get a roll and take it along in case I needed something to chew on along the way. She tried to catch me and take it away but I was much faster than she was. So Mopp gave in and we went jogging with me carrying a roll of toilet paper and Mopp muttering to herself.

After a mile or so, the toilet paper started to interfere a bit with my breathing so I just dropped it. That made Mopp mad. For some reason, she didn't want to leave it in the road and felt it necessary to pick it up and carry it herself. As she was picking it up, I came up close behind her. She turned around too quickly and fell over me. She was lying flat on the road holding this roll of toilet paper as people drove by on their way to work. I could just tell that I was in trouble. When she finally got up (still holding the toilet paper), her hands and knees were bleeding. Actually she looked a bit silly; I tried hard not to laugh and kept a very apologetic, sympathetic expression on my face. When we got home, she spent an hour or so picking pieces of gravel out of her knees and hands and talking to herself. I stayed out of the way, I'm not stupid. Actually, I was exceptionally patient as my breakfast was delayed.

After finally providing my morning sustenance, Mopp got on the phone. I do try not to be critical, but she sounded rather hysterical. She asked her friend Kelly (companion to Hawk) to come over and "take care of me" for one night so she could escape and rest. OK with me. Hawk was my best friend and was always up to a good chase through the woods. Kelly knew where my food and the treats were stored and she was a push-over for extra goodies. So Mopp left for the night. Kelly read books and looked at the talking black box. Hawk and I had a great chase in the woods and came home ready for a good night's sleep. A bit crowded with Kelly, Hawk and I all on the same bed but cozy. When Mopp returned, she described to Kelly her "rest." She had a hot bath, a good dinner without my trying to lick her plate before she was done, an interesting movie, a good night's sleep without my howling in the woods all night, and a good jog without the embarrassment of carrying a roll of toilet paper with bloody hands and knees. Looking pointedly at me, she recounted that she had gotten some peculiar looks when she showed up at a motel with her wrists and knees bandaged. Personally, I think she over-reacted a bit.

Jogging actually turned out to be a great source of food. There were several good—well, adequate—hunting dogs on our normal route. If we managed to get up particularly early, these guys were often still sleeping off their night time activities, and I could quietly help myself to the bones they had left in their yards. Mopp seemed to object to my doing this. I guess she worried that the resident dog would wake up and come after us. I tried to reassure her that I would be happy to protect her. Perhaps, she couldn't understand me with my mouth full of stolen bones because she didn't seem much comforted. If the prize was too much to eat at once, I just took it home with me. Once I managed to get an entire deer leg home from two miles away. That was not easy, especially with Mopp trying to take it away from me for the entire trip. But I am nothing if not stubborn. Another time, I found an entire deer skin—amazing.

I was determined to get the thing home and hide it in the woods. It was not to be. Mopp managed to get that away from me—I kept tripping on it when I was running so she finally caught me, took away the skin and hung it out of reach on a tree branch. Unfair.

One morning's jog turned out to be more exciting than usual. Mopp and I were taking care of Hawken and Sam (a friend of Hawken's) because their humans were away for a few days. Mopp took us all jogging. It was a Sunday morning and very early so we didn't have to worry much about cars—there was only the woman delivering newspapers. We were on our way home. Mopp was leading the pack. The rest of us were lagging behind hoping for some excitement to spring out of the bushes. Then we got lots more excitement than we had anticipated. All of a sudden there was a great big, huge black bull jogging with us. He seemed to think he fit right in. He was just jogging along at the pace we were travelling. He was clearly having a good time. Hawken, Sam and I had no clue as to how to deal with a bull so we pretended he wasn't there and behaved "normally"—well, as normally as possible while staying out of his way and away from his feet. I suppose that was sort of cowardly of us but this guy was as big as a truck.

Mopp hadn't turned around so she had not seen him yet. I was hoping we wouldn't have to protect her. For a few minutes, all five of us just jogged along. The bull got a bit closer to Mopp , and she must have sensed something odd, like his smell. She turned around. Her expression was priceless. She was temporarily speechless. Finally she said, "this is what I get for studying crazy people"—Mopp is a psychologist. She wanted, desperately, to believe she was "seeing things."

When the vision of the bull did not disappear, she wanted to do as we had done—pretend he wasn't there. But how do you do that? This bull was clearly out for a good time and planning to go home with us. I was worried that Mopp might be forced to give him my food—he could eat the whole bag in one bite. Since Mopp had stopped, we all had stopped. She stared at the bull, we stared at the bull. The bull got bored and went to eat some grass. After a few minutes, Mopp took off jogging again calling for us to go with her. She was worried we might get too close to the bull but she did not have to worry about that—we were not dumb. The bull came along still having a great time. If a bull could smile, he had a smile on his face. Finally, we got home. We left the bull outside (thank the goddess) who immediately headed for the garden to help himself to breakfast. Mopp gave us breakfast inside (and we stayed inside) and then she got on the phone. Eventually, she found someone who claimed to know the bull. After the bull had devoured much of the garden while all of us (still being cowards) stared at him out the window, a man with a truck came. The bull seemed delighted to see this man and willingly got into the truck. That was the last time we saw that bull. Mopp talked to herself the rest of the day.

Friends and not-so-Friendly Cats

When I was about a year old and Blair and George were visiting, they came home one afternoon with a baby cat. They walked in, sat down and called me. I wandered over to see what the fuss was about. Mopp held out this squirming thing. My first thought was "great, live dinner tonight." I started to take it into my mouth, but, from Mopp's response, realized this was not supposed to be my dinner. I sniffed again. Well, no big deal. It didn't smell that great anyway, I could handle letting it live. Big mistake. Soon there were five of these things—Sadie, Clementine, Hester, Thoby, and Oliver. They actually lived in the house with us and used the doggy door. So they were everywhere, running all over the place. I did not appreciate their ability to climb up on top of everything. I never knew when one was hanging about up above watching me. They could also climb trees. I particularly disliked that probably because I was jealous. If a coonhound could climb trees, imagine!!!!!

Blair and George introducing me to my first baby cat

Although I never came to actually like cats, I did manage to tolerate, and occasionally, appreciate, them. They were, afterall, not entirely stupid so they were trainable. Sometimes, they would walk underneath me and rub against my legs. Sort of gave me the creeps but what can you expect from a cat. At first I thought they were trying to get my food but Mopp said they were just showing affection. Wierd!! In my house, cats had to learn three things. The first was to never, never, never come closer than 3 feet in any direction while I was sleeping; there was nothing worse than being abruptly awakened out of a wonderful dream because some dumb cat stepped on my foot or sniffed my tail. The second was never, never, never approach my food although I eventually relented on sharing my water bowl. And the third was any "catch" was to be given to me as a tribute to my superiority. Sometimes, one of them caught a mouse or mole or bird and was more than happy to supplement my diet when the choice was to give me the catch or die.

Better yet, I was occasionally awakened by loud gagging noises. Cats do not throw up quietly. I learned that this horrible noise often meant a great dessert. I had to be quick in order to beat Mopp to it. I didn't mind when she got the hair ball ones— yuck. But they would often throw up recently eaten food which was quite tasty. Although she never thanked me, Mopp should have been grateful for my training the cats. Occasionally, one of the cats decided to give Mopp a "gift" and leave a little tidbit (like a mouse head) on the floor next to the bed or even on top of the bed. If I didn't get to these first, Mopp found them. She clearly did not appreciate the gift especially if she stepped on it with her bare feet as she got out of bed.

Clementine, the white cat, was the source of a rather severe embarrassment for me. I liked cat food so Mopp put the cat food bowls up on shelves so the cats could jump up and get to it but I couldn't reach it. When Clementine was a baby and couldn't yet jump, Mopp devised one her endless little creative gadgets. She made up a little cage with Clementine's food and water. She fixed it so that the door opened only far enough for dumb little Clementine to get through. Obviously the opening was not big enough for a 75 pound coonhound. When Mopp saw me drooling around the little cage, she said that that was precisely the point of the little door—so that I couldn't get Clementine's food. That cat food smelled SO good, I couldn't stand it.

One night, around 3 AM, I decided to figure out how to get the cat food out of that cage. I messed around for a bit with the latch and finally got it open. I stuck my head into the cage and ate the food—great stuff. When I finished, I tried to get my head out but the cage was stuck. I panicked. With this stupid cage on my head, I couldn't see anything, I couldn't tell where I was. I started running around in circles, banging against furniture. The cat water spilled all over my head. Mopp woke up—not a big surprise. When she saw me, she sat down and laughed and laughed and laughed. I failed to see the humor. Eventually, she gained control of herself and removed the cage from my head. I gave up on cat food, well, temporarily anyway.

I had heard from friends that cat poop was rather tasty. Inside the house, Mopp had set up the kitty litter in a closet with a cat-size hole in the wall so I couldn't get to it. But one fine day, I woke from a nap in the garden to find Thoby (the orange cat) digging a hole nearby and then pooping into it. As soon as he was gone, I dug it up for breakfast dessert. Mopp didn't have a category called "breakfast dessert" so I had to find my own. As it turned out, cat poop didn't "sit well" in my stomach. After a few days of following cats around outside, I reluctantly gave it up. I suppose it was for the best. Mopp wouldn't kiss me with cat poop smell on my breath. I might add that I never did tire of cat vomit—that was great. My final analysis of cats was that they're OK—but "just." They have their uses but they should be trained early and trained well.

I can't say that the cats were truly friends—more like barely tolerated house mates. But I had wonderful dog friends. Many of Mopp's people friends lived with dogs, and they usually came to visit together. The humans would eat and talk, and the dogs and I would go off into the woods to hunt or scrounge or annoy raccoons. I usually enjoyed myself when Mopp's friends brought their dogs over to our house. Those who were bright enough to figure out the doggy door (you wouldn't think it would take too many brains to figure that out—it is called the "doggy" door) could be pleasant companions for a walk or hunt. With one exception, they all learned quickly that I am "in charge," any available food is mine, and I get first choice of sleeping spots. The one exception was a Great Dane. I won't go into that. Suffice it to say, that I liked dogs, other than the Great Dane, to visit and I enjoyed visiting their houses. Sometimes dog friends came to stay here for a few days or even a few weeks when their people couldn't take care of them for some reason. After I trained them on the rules, they behaved well enough. I enjoyed the company for awhile but was always glad to see them go and have Mopp and my house to myself again.

A few times, when Mopp wasn't at home, Jill and Lana came over and wanted me to leave with them in their car. I thought this was strange but I knew they were Mopp's friends and that she trusted them so they were my friends as well. AND they took my food bowl and a bag of food from the kitchen so what choice did I have. I couldn't let them leave with my food. Jill and Lana didn't know how to put the window down with the air conditioner on. As it turned out, they just took me home with them and fed me. They have three dogs, four cats, and two rabbits—never a dull moment. Jill and Lana were very nice to me but they wouldn't let me eat the rabbits. Then Mopp came over later to pick me up and take me home again. Mopp apparently ate her dinner elsewhere.

Of all my dog friends, Hawken was my favorite. His person, Kelly, worked long hours and sometimes had to leave home for a few days, so Hawken spent a lot of time at our house. He was great. When we got a meal, Mopp stood guard so I couldn't intimidate him and convince him to give me his food. But he always left just a little bit for me. Hawken was always ready and willing for a chase or a hunt no matter what time of day or night. But Hawken and I had different goals. He "pointed" and "stalked"—he tried to be very, very quiet so he could sneak up on potential food whereas I wanted to chase and track with as much noise as I could muster. So he was often rather disgusted with my behavior but always joined in for the chase. Of course, we never caught anything—the woods just cleared out as soon as I opened my mouth but occasionally we found dead stuff. Hawken would help me carry it back home and hide it so Mopp wouldn't find it. Fortunately, Hawken had a tendency to save goodies for "a rainy day." Not me, rainy days were just uncomfortable jogging days as far as I was concerned so I usually dug up and ate the share he was "saving" after he went home.

Occasionally, our different hunting strategies served us well. Frequently, Mopp drove us to a huge lake for a long walk. There were lots of ducks on the lake and lots of people who came to give the ducks bread. Bread is, of course, one of my favorites. When Hawken and I came across a group of ducks eating bread, Hawken chased the ducks into the water while I ate their bread. Hawken had great fun swimming after those ducks but he never got one. I didn't have to get wet and I got the bread. Over the years, Kelly adopted other dogs so Necco, Abbie, and Sampson lived with Hawk and became my friends. They lived about a mile from here. When their people were at work, they sometimes made their way over here, plowed through the doggy door and napped with me on Mopp's bed.

Preparing to nap with Necco and Hawken

George and Blair were two of my favorite human friends. They were visiting when I "arrived." They visited every summer and sometimes in the winter. Wonderful friends. They didn't come with a dog so I got all the attention and got to lick everyone's plate. But, when I was a few years old, they arrived for their yearly visit and had a dog with them—Bergen, a little Chinese boy with a wrinkled up face. I felt betrayed. They had never come with a dog before. Before Bergen, I got all the treats and all the toys. So I, of course, put up a fuss and expected them to get rid of him. I screamed, howled, yelled, barked—there was no question about my feelings on the subject. I just kept howling and planned to do so until they took him away. I didn't try to hurt him or anything—I might have if he had gone for my food. I think my voice scared him which is exactly what I meant to do. Mopp was actually planning to let him sleep in my house. So I just kept howling. Eventually, I got tired and my throat hurt. But it was clear that Mopp, Blair, and George were not going to budge on this one. Mopp promised that he had brought his own food and his own bed and that, if I behaved and stopped howling, maybe he would give me a little of his food. I shut up. Why didn't she tell me that initially. I didn't know he had brought food. Well, eventually I got used to Bergen and learned to "play well with others" as Mopp put it. Well, whatever, Bergen had his own people, he wasn't about to move in. As long as he understood that I was in charge and that he was to stay away from my food, I could tolerate him.

Blair and George stored Bergen's bag of food in a closet. I knew it was in there—I could smell it but with three humans wandering around, I couldn't get it. One day, the three of them left Bergen and me at home alone while they left to do some human thing. This was my chance. I snuck into the closet. I couldn't find the food. I nosed around and then realized that they had put the bag up on a high shelf so I couldn't reach it.

Oh well, I tried. I turned around to leave the closet and realized that in all my scrounging around looking for the food, I had pushed the door closed and I was stuck in that silly closet with the food completely out of reach. Of all the embarrassing and frustrating situations. After a few hours, Blair, George, and Mopp came home. I kept quiet. When Mopp didn't see me, she called. And she called and she called. Then she started getting worried. It was dinner time and she knew there would have to something terribly wrong for me to be absent for dinner. This was one dilemma in which my superior brain power was not going to provide a solution. I gave in. I barked and gave a little howl. They found me, and, immediately, understood what had happened. They laughed and laughed. Humans have a weird sense of humor.

Bergen lived with us once for 6 months because Blair and George had to go to France. Apparently, Bergen wasn't allowed in France, maybe because he is Chinese. So I got to know him a bit better. Initially, he came across as rather stupid but, once I got to know him a bit better, I realized he wasn't stupid—only impulsive. He knew after he did something stupid that it was stupid—he just couldn't help himself. Once he was "missing" and Mopp found him on the big road with all the cars; he was just running around in circles—a bit hard to understand the motivation. Another time, a whole group of us persons and dogs went for a long walk. At the end of the walk was a house with some huge Malamutes chained up in the backyard. We all knew better than to go near the place but Bergen just ran into the yard and started to harass these guys. Mopp asked someone to hold on to me so I wouldn't follow her (fat chance, Malamutes are dangerous) and went to rescue him. Over the years, I did adjust to Bergen's visits and we became good friends. We just had to learn to accept and appreciate each other's idiosyncrasies. I did draw the line, however, at sharing a car seat with him. He wiggled too much. So when they visited and we all went out in the car, Blair, George and Bergen sat in the back seat, Mopp drove, and I got the passenger seat—with the window open and the air conditioner on.

Food, Food, and Snacks

Over the years, I have had to develop multiple strategies to satisfy my appetite. Mopp's idea of nutrition may have been "healthy" but it wasn't much fun. In pursuit of special food treats, I not only benefited from my height, but also my nonchalant attitude that put people off-guard, and my incredibly quick actions. I could grab and be out the doggy door in a second. I got a whole chunk of brie cheese from Chris, an entire dinner from Val, and numerous, numerous loaves of bread. I loved bread, especially the stuff Mopp made.

About once a month in the summer, Mopp invited a bunch of people over for an outdoor dinner. When dinner time started to approach, Mopp brought food and plates outside to the picnic table. At some point in these preparations, she brought out a freshly baked loaf of bread, put it in the middle of the table, and said to those gathered around the picnic table, "would all of you keep on eye on the bread, Emma will try to steal it—please don't let her." Everyone turned and looked at me and I managed to look innocent and adorable with food being the last thing on my mind. Then Mopp went back inside to cook or something and all the people forgot about the bread and returned to some silly human behavior like talking. It was like taking a chew hoove from a newly born puppy. I just casually walked up to the table, put my front paws on the bench, took the bread very quietly in my mouth, and left for the woods. No one, and I mean no one even noticed. These people were all so busy talking and so, so interested in talking that they didn't pay attention to anything else. Over the years, Mopp learned to bake two loaves of bread. She recognized my superiority and accepted her defeat in this matter.

Fisher people were an unusually good source of tantalizing treats. Some of Mopp's friends liked to catch fish in the lake. This was fine with Mopp. So occasionally someone or a group or a whole family came over for a few hours and sat on the lake shore or took the boat out to go fishing. And sometimes they brought their lunch. Not knowing the dangers of doing so, they left their lunch bag on the ground until they were hungry. I didn't even have to reach. I just strolled by, picked up the bag, strode off into the woods, and indulged. At times, I had to scrounge through some silly fruit but there was always a sandwich, often potato chips, and occasionally a chocolate dessert. Eventually the regulars caught on and kept their lunch bag out of reach but there were always new fisher people who didn't know my skills. Because Mopp was nice enough to let them fish, they never complained to her and she never learned of this.

A few times a year, Mopp had her students here for lunch. She usually had cheese, bread, green stuff, and chocolate cake—other than the green stuff, a great menu for me. There were usually lots of people, like 20. They filled up a plate with food and found a place to sit on the floor or outside on the deck. And Mopp told everyone before lunch, "Emma will try to steal your food if you put it on the floor. You can't put your food on the floor even for a second so be careful." At first, I objected to this. I considered this cheating on Mopp's part but then I found that it didn't matter. I could get just about anything I wanted. Even after her little speech, they still put their food on the floor for a second and that was all it took—one second. And with 20 people spread out on two floors and lots of rooms, I could get quite a bit before a general alarm was raised. Mopp was agreeable to my licking everyone's plates. Licking paper plates is a learned skill. I had to hold it down with one foot so it didn't slide away.

Chocolate cake was the real challenge. By the time dessert rolled around, everyone eyed me with suspicion and everyone loved Mopp's chocolate cake so they did not even leave crumbs. Only once did I get my fill of chocolate cake. Mopp invited some friends over for tea and cake. They were all out on the porch and Mopp, with a suspicious eye on me, had put the cake smack in the middle of her huge sewing table to cool. There was no way I could reach it by putting my front paws up on the table. I could smell it, I knew it was there and so close. It was just sitting there—so perfect. Mopp and her friends were out of sight. Very, very, very quietly, I leaped up on top of the table. I waited a second, no one heard me. So I ate, and ate, and ate. Before I had finished the whole thing, however, Mopp walked in. I could tell I was in trouble. I thought it best to leave for awhile. When I returned, there were no visitors and no cake. Mopp said, "I thought you'd come back in time for dinner." She was right, of course.

As I mentioned before, Mopp and I had come to an agreement about the special treats I found in the woods. I had to keep it outside or lose it. That worked in the summer. But then winter came. Coon hounds are not designed for cold, snowy, icy conditions. Unfortunately, some of the best stuff was available after hunting season—so December and January had great pickings but this was not the best weather to spend hours outside chewing. Well, I learned from Mopp to look for creative solutions. I brought the tidbit indoors when Mopp was upstairs, then quickly turned around and started to go back out but stopped in the middle of the doggy door. I figured out how to lie down with my body in the heated house and my head outside. I could chew to my heart's content and still keep most of me warm. Mopp was not impressed, nor was she amused. She tried to grab the food but I just picked it up and left since I was half way out the door already. Mopp said I was letting in all the cold air from outside. I understood that but I didn't see that as a problem. The house was still warm. She also complained that the cats couldn't use the doggy door with my fat butt blocking it. My butt was not fat. And who cares about cats. Since Mopp didn't have much choice, she let me do that for one winter but the next summer she built an outdoor passage to the doggy door. Then if I tried to keep my body inside, Mopp went outside and grabbed the treat before I could run through the passage and away. She won that round. After that, I indulged outside until I was cold and numb, ran back in to get warm, went back outside to chew, and so on. The treats did last longer this way but it was lots of work for a member of a breed that has a reputation for being lazy.

Eventually, my reputation for having a rather voracious appetite extended far and wide. Can't deny that, it was true. But as a "reputation", it could be embarrassing. One sunny, beautiful afternoon Mopp, Jill, Lana, and Denise (people) along with Maggie, Muffy, and I (dogs) went for a walk around a large lake on the campus at the university. Mopp and I often went for walks with this group. An interesting digression: I was a large dog, about 75 pounds and Muffy was a little thing, about 10 pounds. So when we met other people, they never approached me making endearing sounds but approached the cute little Muffy. Ironically, I wouldn't dream of biting anyone while Muffy would as soon take a chunk out of some one as have a biscuit. Our people were constantly having to warn strangers not to touch Muffy but they offered me to the little kids who "wanted to pet the doggie." Few took them up on it.

Back to the story. We were a big group so no one was paying much attention—the women, as usual, were talking, talking, talking (this obsession people have with language—they miss so much of the really important stuff). So when I smelled something superb, I followed my nose. It led me across a street. I felt a twinge of guilt because I'm not supposed to cross a street by myself—but just a twinge. The smell was overpowering. My nose led me behind a large building. There were a bunch of men grilling and eating steaks. These guys were great, they were not vegetarians. Well, I certainly found the place to be on this beautiful, sunny afternoon. I looked as sad and lost and hungry as a slightly overweight Treeing Walker Coonhound is able and, predictably, they started giving me snacks. I decided to hang around awhile. They offered me some beer but I turned that down.

In the meantime, as I found out later, someone in the walking group finally noticed I wasn't there. They yelled, shouted, screamed and then split in two groups with one going in one direction, the other in the other direction trying to find me. Going around the lake, one group noticed a large and wonderful looking half sandwich sitting in the middle of the path. Denise said, "Emma has not been this way, she would never have passed that up." She was correct, of course, but how embarrassing to have that kind of reputation. When Mopp and I eventually found each other, she grabbed me, hugged me, kissed me; she was crying a bit. I was just a little bit ashamed of myself. I hadn't meant to upset Mopp, I just wanted that steak.

Mopp told me once that my stealing food off the counter at every opportunity made it difficult to recruit critter sitters. The first few times that Mopp had to leave for a few days, I worried that my critter sitter wouldn't know where the food was or how much I was supposed to get. But Mopp trained them well and I always got my standard fare. Actually, these were times of particularly good opportunities for more and better food. Mopp didn't go away often and never for long—a week at the most. Although I didn't like her to leave, the guilt she felt about leaving me was useful. The day before she left town, we went for a "special" walk, I got a "special" dinner, and, after being smothered with hugs, kisses, squeezes, I got a couple of extra biscuits. Then, when Mopp returned, I got another "special" dinner. And she always brought me a present. I always appreciated the present but the present could have been bigger and better if she didn't waste her money on cat presents.

When new to the job, the sitter didn't appreciate my counter surfing abilities. As usual, Mopp always warned them to never leave their food unattended, but they always forgot until they learned the hard way to appreciate my speed and skill. I was able to get lots of great food—lasagna one night, chocolate cake another night. Some of them even bar-b-qued. I learned the painful lesson at a very young age, that stuff off the grill burned my mouth. But, I experimented and found that, if I was very, very careful, I could hold the food in my teeth with my lips curled back so it wouldn't burn. Then I ran off into the woods and had a great snack when it cooled off. Several of the sitters actually bar-b-qued good stuff like chicken and cow, not like Mopp who only grilled soy bean junk and veges—yuck.

These folks were pretty smart for people. If I licked and licked and licked the bottom of my bowl and stared at them as if they had misunderstood the instructions, they assumed they hadn't given me enough food and gave me more. All I had to do was look at the biscuit container with a certain, mournful expression, and I got a biscuit. One sitter caught me at my trick of smacking a plate at the back of the counter so that the food would fly up and into my mouth. She was so impressed that she demonstrated this to her friends when they came over and, of course, the demonstration had to include food of some sort so I got even more. Some of sitters didn't go jogging in the morning. That left me a bit up-in-the-air with my schedule but I could handle that. I, of course, preferred Mopp—she and I were a perfect team—but there were compensations for her absences. I did always greet her appropriately when she came home and gave me presents.

Party Girl

Oh, did I love parties!!! Many of my people and dog friends came together for my yearly birthday party. The early birthdays were the best. The first year there were about 12 dog friends and 15 people friends. Those dogs who figured out the doggy door were quite funny. They apparently thought that going in and out and in and out was the most fun they had had in years. It was regular parade. Some of the labs interspersed swimming between going in and out which made quite a mess that Mopp had to clean up but a party is a party—of course a mess was the result. The people made up contests for the dogs. I thought this a bit unfair. I should have made up the contests and the rules—it was my birthday. But we had to "sit and stay," retrieve a ball, catch a frizbee in the air, find a hidden toy, sing (the singing was awful, particularly the singing that the people did in order to get their dogs to sing).

One year there was even a costume contest. I refused to participate but I did appreciate the bull dog in the tutu. The dog that won each contest got a prize. The prizes were individually-sized cakes made from hot dogs and meat toddler foods. Great stuff. BUT I don't chase balls, catch frizbees, or any of those other silly things—I'm a coonhound. I wanted all those cakes and had no intention of being in some silly contest to get them. I DO know how to manipulate a crowd and I know how to cause a diversion. And it was my birthday, after all. I managed to get about half of them while attention was on the contests. Mopp said "just because you are bigger and smarter than everyone else, it doesn't mean you can take food away from them." I don't see why not. Just to keep Mopp appeased, I decided that next year I would let those who brought me a really good birthday present have their own cake. Fair's fair. But one of Mopp's rules for the succeeding parties was no food. At least the people continued to bring me presents although some of these weren't particularly my kind of thing. Who needs a ball? Who needs a squeaky toy? Well, sometimes I did like squeaky toys, and I can't say that I didn't enjoy ripping the innards out of a stuffed raccoon. One year, Jill and Lana gave me a pair of goggles to keep the bug out of my eyes.

Where is my motorcycle?

One year we planned to have a Thanksgiving party. People, some with dog companions, came from far away. And, of course, Kelly and Hawken were invited. Mopp even gave up being a vegetarian for a day and got a real turkey so the cooking smells were tantalizing. Unfortunately, a tragedy interfered with our plans. Most of the guests were here, dinner was ready, and we were waiting for Kelly and Hawken. Kelly called and said that Hawken was missing. Her neighbor, a horrible person, had often complained about Hawken being on his property. Kelly was worried that the neighbor had somehow hurt Hawken. Emma to the rescue!! All the people and all the dogs drove over there. Mopp said to me, "Find Hawken." Thank the goddess for my superb nose. I took off and tracked Hawken through the woods between her house and that of the nasty neighbor. I found him lying down at the bottom of a big hill. He was obviously hurt. I howled and howled until all the people came. They carried him back to Kelly's house and she took him to the doctor. He had been shot by a shotgun. The vet was able to fix him up and he was fine. Unfortunately, he had to spend the night in the hospital and didn't get any turkey. And I was a heroine!!!!! A few days later on our morning jog, I stopped and left a little pile in the middle of the nasty neighbor's highly manicured lawn.

Finishing up Thanksgiving dinner

A year or so later, Kelly and Jerry decided to get married and to get married in my yard by the lake. This was going to be a great party. A few days before the wedding, Mopp and Kelly made a huge, huge, huge wedding cake. The kitchen was filled with flour, sugar, eggs, butter, chocolate. The butter or chocolate would have been worth some effort but Mopp knew enough to keep those away from me. I was becoming very frustrated with my "take." There was too much food around to just give up. I was allowed to lick the bowls after they were already empty but this was not satisfying. There was so much food, the counters were full so they put a carton of eggs on the floor. I had had eggs before, they were OK, they would do in a pinch—a coonhound living with a vegetarian is hard to imagine but there I was and had to adjust. So I grabbed the carton of eggs and made a dash for the doggy door. The carton opened up and eggs started falling out and breaking all over the floor. I turned around and tried to eat them quickly before Mopp grabbed me. I needn't have worried. Mopp and Kelly were sitting on the floor and laughing hysterically. I think they were enjoying a little wine while baking. I did not find it all that funny. Food is not a laughing matter. I did get most of the eggs.

The wedding. What a feast. Mopp made ruffled collars for Hawken, Necco, Sampson, and I to match Kelly's wedding dress. I felt a little silly being a coonhound and all but the ruffles didn't look so bad after we got them wet and dirty. We all had a good time, lots of food dropped here and there, lots of food to just grab while walking past a table. But after awhile, boredom set in. After they ate, the people just talked and talked. Boring. So my three buddies and I took off for the woods and we found a feast—most of a deer. There was plenty to go around—we each got a huge portion—I got the rib cage, Hawken got the spinal cord, Necco got a whole leg and Sampson got something I couldn't identify and we trotted happily back to the wedding carrying our booty. By the time we returned, most of the people had left. When Mopp saw us, she was not pleased but she did appreciate that we had not brought back old dead deer parts while all the guests were still there.

We were supposed to go to something called a "reception" and Mopp had been left in charge of getting us all there. First, of course, she threw all of our booty into the lake. Those fish must have loved me for all that I donated to their diet. Then she tried to get all four of us and her into the cab of her truck. It was a tight, tight squeeze made possible only by the fact that Hawken preferred the floor. After about 10 minutes of riding, I started to feel a bit queasy. I think maybe that spinal cord was a bit "old." Another few minutes and I couldn't help it, I lost my wedding lunch. I aimed down toward the floor only realizing too late that Hawken—my best friend in the whole world—was on the floor. I felt so bad—both my stomach and my conscience for throwing up all over Hawken. He actually didn't seem to mind too much but Mopp groaned very loudly. She managed to stop the truck. She got Hawken out, cleaned him up as well as possible, gave me a dirty look, put Hawken back inside and off we went to the reception where there was more food. What a day.

Road Kill and Dairy Queen

Treeing Walker Coonhounds are "supposed to" track and tree raccoons. Once the raccoons are up a tree, the job becomes howling very loudly so that a human can find you and shoot the raccoon. And, for some reason, maybe because most humans "go to work" during the day, these tracking/hunting/shooting activities take place at night—in the middle of the night. Lucky me, I did not live the typical coonhound life. Running around in the woods at night was great but only if I was awake and in the mood, it was not raining, and it was not terribly cold. And guns make a scary noise. Usually, my nights were reserved for sleeping in a quiet, comfortable, temperature-controlled bed—on top of the quilt in the summer, under the quilt in the winter.

My day typically started at dawn. I stood, stretched, got rid of the accumulated gas and wandered outside. I strolled around the barn and the car to see if anyone was around, to ensure the safety of my buried treasures, and to make sure the cats were behaving. There was usually some activity in the woods but I ignored it. This wasn't a good time to get involved in a chase. Mopp liked me to be "around" and be prepared to jog. A little later, Mopp got up and went through the lengthy morning ritual of putting clothes on. She was so slow in the morning and took forever. I usually got impatient and started down the driveway before she was ready. When she finally got outside, I was already half way down the drive. Early days, Mopp just stood there and called and called and called for me. I had to come all the way back home so she could see me. Although a bit slow to learn, Mopp eventually realized, that if I wasn't there, to just start out and I would be waiting for her down the road.

Then we set off for our run. We had two routes—Mopp's favorite started out going past Rocky (a yippie, hyper, macho-type boxer) who barked and barked and barked. He was completely harmless but still annoying. His bark pierced the early morning quiet. Mopp frequently commented that we should stuff a sock in his mouth. Next we came to the home of Shep (Collie) and Digby (Jack Russel). They were nice but somewhat boring. Mopp always stopped to pet them but I tended to ignore them unless they had their birds with them. Shep and Digby lived with chickens, quineas, and turkeys. That boy turkey was so interesting but didn't have a brain in his head. He strutted around in the middle of the road like he didn't know what a car was. The chickens were fun. Mopp let me walk around them but yelled if I chased them. Last came Cricket and Mace (Australian sheep dogs) and Huckleberry. Cricket and Mace were kind of useless in the absence of sheep but Huckleberry was a mutt and a very smart, sophisticated mutt. He always had good eats, like small dead mammals or deer parts, in his front yard. Unfortunately he wasn't generous. Fortunately, he was often not home and I could just help myself.

On the way home, Mopp often stopped and talked to one of the neighbors. This delayed my breakfast. I tried, unsuccessfully to make her feel guilty. When we finally got home, my breakfast was prepared first. I always got breakfast before the cats., Mopp gave the cats some canned cat food in the morning. If I was quick and Mopp wasn't watching, I could always intimidate at least one of the cats and get their food. Mopp tried feeding them on the counters to prevent this but I could usually reach the bowls without too much trouble. Mopp had trouble keeping watch over five cats. After the cats were done, I got to lick all the cat bowls—Thoby always left a little for me while Oliver licked his so clean there was barely a scent of food (I got him later). Then it was time to fill the dry cat food bowls. For some reason, Mopp had trouble remembering to do this so I had to stand in front of one of the bowls until she noticed me and remembered. If you have read this far, you are probably surprised that I would go to all this trouble to ensure the cats got fed. Well, I got a small handful of dry cat food when Mopp filled the bowls.

One bright and beautiful Sunday morning, we were jogging along and I smelled something simply tantalizing. After investigating, I found a recently road-killed rabbit. Great. I sat down to breakfast. Mopp, clearly prone to hysteria, went ballistic. I had to keep picking the rabbit up and moving it as she ran after me obviously trying to get it for herself. I found it. She could go find her own breakfast. Eventually, she calmed down a bit. She said (in a highly exaggerated voice) that she was going home and I could come home when it suited me. Well, those instructions were just fine with me. Great breakfast. I wandered into the house an hour or so later—very proud of myself and looking forward to my regular breakfast. Mopp was in a bad mood. I could tell she wasn't thinking about preparing my breakfast. I followed her around hinting, hinting, hinting. Finally she gave me my breakfast but rather grudgingly I thought. We settled down to the morning routine—she worked, I napped. But everytime I woke up, Mopp gave me a dirty look. What was going on? Finally, after several hours, she sat down with me and explained that she would forgive me because I was only doing what was "natural." I wasn't impressed. Forgive me for what? I didn't do anything wrong. Everything I ever did was natural except ride in cars, have baths, go to school and go to the doctor and none of those were my idea. She was just jealous because I got the rabbit before she did.

A bit later, Mopp suggested we go into town to Dairy Queen for lunch. I think she realized that she had been jealous and had been unfair to me. And I love Dairy Queen—what a treat. We got into the car and started into town. The motion of the car going up and down hills and around corners started to make me feel a bit queasy. Maybe my stomach wasn't quite used to whole rabbit as a breakfast appetizer. Well, I couldn't help it, I threw up all over the car seat. My first thought was, "no big deal, we are on our way to lunch anyway. I may as well have an empty stomach." Mopp didn't quite see it that way. She stopped the car and just sat there and stared ahead for a long time. I got into the back seat. I didn't like sitting on a soggy, messy car seat getting vomit on my feet. Mopp found some towels and tried to clean up the seat but not enough for me to want to get up front again. The smell was better in the back seat. She mumbled something about "natural" and talked to herself all the way to Dairy Queen. I used to have trouble deciding if I wanted a cone or a cup. A cone is more food, a cup can be ripped to shreds after lunch. Mopp solved my dilemma by ordering a cone in a cup. Was I spoiled or what?

The Human Animal

I lived with Mopp and loved her, but I never truly understood her or any other humans. They spent time and effort on activities that did not seem to have anything to do with food or fun—so what was the point?? Mopp did something she called "work." I did accept that she had to do this so she could buy stuff like dog food and snacks but I didn't understand the "why." Often she left for a few hours or the whole day to go to "work." Occasionally, she "worked" at home. Part of "work" was talking on the telephone. I listened to her phone conversations when she was at home—at least I tried to listen. At times they were so incredibly boring that I could barely stay awake. She also chatted on the phone to her human friends. The mention of "bath" or "vet" woke me up immediately and I was out the doggy door and gone for the rest of the day. Mopp eventually realized I understood and stopped announcing to her friends any unpleasant activities she had planned for me. For awhile she tried spelling "bath" and "vet" but I learned that any spelling meant I wasn't going to like what was coming, and the best course was to hang out in the woods for awhile.

Another quirk of humans is their compulsion to clean everything. I guess I can understand Mopp giving me a bath if I am coated with dead fish scales or raccoon poop--she does not recognize this as my accessorizing. But to bathe me just to get rid of a smell she happens not to like??? The fragrance that I am able to achieve occasionally is enough to make me feel how Mopp looks like she feels after a bit too much wine. Truly wonderful. And who invented a vacuum cleaner? They are noisy and scoop up all the good smells and food crumbs. And laundry. Just when I get my beds, couches, and futons nice and sweet smelling, off they go to the laundry.

Because most of Mopp's friends lived with dogs, and sometimes even cats, Mopp and her friends often discussed the differences between human animals and non-human animals. After years of listening to Mopp's conversations and years of living with Mopp, I realized that the human animal believed that coonhounds (and any non-human animals) did not and could not understand human language. They believed that we could understand "simple" words like "sit," "stay," but that any bunch of words was too much for our little brains. The truth of the matter has, I believe, never occurred to a human—we can understand but the content of what humans say is so utterly boring and irrelevant, that we do not attend and do not respond. We respond to "sit" and "stay" because, if we don't, we wind up back in "school." Those of us who have made the mistake of letting our human partners know we can understand language have regretted it the rest of our lives. The truly pathetic result of confessing to understanding English was that, thereafter, the humans never, never, never shut up. They chattered all day long and expected their coonhound to pay attention to all their trivia. The human animal is so addicted to this frivolous behavior that they even have boxes that talk when they get tired.

I should not have been so critical of this human failing. I did understand why human animals are so obsessed with talking. They must do their best with what they've got and they don't have much. Since they can't smell much, their lives must be very, very boring. They can't track or hunt or get enjoyment out of just sniffing the air. They can't see very well so they miss a lot when going for walks in the woods. They can't sleep all day because they have to "work." They can't even go outside in cold weather without spending 10 minutes messing around with clothes and boots, and they don't like hot weather. One can hardly blame them for getting so bent out of shape over language. It is all they have going for them.

With Mopp

In the typical household, there is not much verbal communication between human animals and their animal partners. The human animals assume their four-legged companions do not understand and, even if humans tried to communicate, the non-human animals stop listening because they get bored with the boring topics that human animals talk about. Mopp and I probably had more verbal communication than most human-coonhound pairs because Mopp did not live with another human. So when she had something to say, she said it to me. More accurately, when she wanted to talk, she talked to me—she didn't always have something to say when she talked. And, probably, she often just used me as an excuse to talk to herself especially when she was trying to solve a problem or understand another human or understand me. And Mopp and I probably had more communication than other pairs because we lived in the same house. Coonhounds forced to live outside in the cold, apart from their human companions wouldn't have much opportunity to learn a language. But, even Mopp, much as I loved her and thought she was a great coonhound companion, did not understand that I understood. I once heard her say to another human, "sometimes Emma seems to understand language." This probably occurred to her when I disappeared after hearing "bath" mentioned. Actually, I didn't understand much language because it was just too boring to pay enough attention to learn it all. But I understood as much as I needed or wanted. It was because I understood language that I was able to slip off into the woods with a loaf of bread or look pathetic when Mopp was about to take a trip and, thereby, get extra treats or make sure I got a good night's sleep before a visit from Hawken.

From listening to Mopp's phone conversations and to various voices from the box, I came to the astonishing conclusion that humans believe they have superior intelligence because they talk. They think that they are smarter simply because they talk—regardless of what they say. The obvious question is, "why, in the face of all the contradictory evidence, would they believe that?" Perhaps, because humans are so handicapped in most areas, this is their only way to improve their self-esteem. Unfortunately, coonhounds have to work harder than they would ordinarily have to because humans are so stupid.

Let me give one simple example of the many instances of this. Although Mopp and I loved each other and enjoyed each other's company, there were many activities we couldn't do together—well, we could have, I suppose, but we chose not to. I chose not to go "to work" with Mopp. "Work" was really and truly boring other than checking out all the wastebaskets for discarded food which took 108 seconds. And Mopp chose not to hunt with me in the middle of the night. But activities we both enjoyed, we did together. Hiking we both enjoyed and did this together but as soon as Mopp couldn't see me (and she couldn't see very far), she didn't know where I was and started yelling. I always knew where she was even if I couldn't see her because I could smell her and, if I couldn't smell her, I could always track her by smell. So who was smarter? Being the more intelligent, I had to be the one to solve this little problem. As soon as she started calling and scaring all the wildlife away, I knew she wouldn't shut up until she could see me. So I learned to come back close enough for her to see me (and I had to get close) and then she was fine. Sometimes she even got the direction wrong—she would look off in the opposite direction and call me. Sometimes, just as a little coonhound joke, I would come back quietly and sit down right behind her. She didn't know I was there until she turned around and essentially tripped over me. She'd laugh, the way people laugh when they do something stupid. I tried to be understanding about her low IQ but sometimes it was a bit much. I won't mention the stupidity of jogging in the middle of a thunder storm or in 16 inches of snow or the logic of giving me a bath or sitting in front of a talking black box for hours.

Actually, I believed just the opposite—the reason humans are so stupid is because of this language thing. Humans thought they got a good thing going with their enlarged brains but they didn't count on the language tumor. The language tumor grew and grew and wiped out most of the brain parts for smell, sight, and basic logic. So they have huge brains that do them little good because so much of their brains are senselessly used up by language. Can you imagine what they would be capable of if their language brain parts were devoted, instead, to smell or sight? And, more importantly, can you imagine what they would be capable of if they didn't waste their time messing around with language—reading, writing, talking, listening— there is no end to the silly human fascination with language. And, to top it off, humans aren't all that good at it. Once, when Mopp was dragging me into the shower for a bath, I tried to tell her that not all dogs had to have baths, that giving me baths was not necessary for her to be a good coonhound companion. Her response was, "no one who rolls in a very dead raccoon is going to sleep in my bed without a bath." You would think that a member of a species so obsessed with spoken language would know not to say "very dead." But Mopp did, as always, get her point across one way or another. I wanted to sleep in her bed so….

I tried and tried to teach Mopp but she was never an easy student. Once I overheard a conversation Mopp was having with a friend—again, the topic was the difference between human and coonhound intelligence. The friend said that one of the criteria for intelligence is the ability to deceive (I would agree) but then this person said that coonhounds aren't capable of deception. I laughed and laughed and laughed—Mopp thought I was choking and massaged my throat. Well, I felt an obligation to educate her—such extreme ignorance is probably dangerous. Hawken was visiting, and when Mopp came home from work, he was limping a little. He had stepped on a thorn that afternoon, and he hadn't been able to dig it out with his teeth. Mopp noticed and petted him and then took the thorn out. She then gave him a special treat. While this was going on, I was virtually ignored. So, to prove I could deceive Mopp, I limped around a little, pretending to be hurt. Then I got some attention, had my foot checked; no thorn but I did get a special treat. I looked appropriately grateful for the treat and then, without limping, tore out the doggy door after an intruding opossum. I thought that was pretty clear deception but Mopp wasn't bright enough to "get it."

I had to try again. And, again, I planned this for when Hawken was visiting. When Mopp ate her dinner, she gave us biscuits. She put a few down for Hawken and then gave me my biscuits on the other side of the room so I couldn't grab Hawken's biscuits. Of course, I wanted my biscuits AND Hawken's biscuits. So I ate my biscuits quickly and then went over to the window and started barking hysterically and howling. Hawken, thinking I was barking at something interesting, dashed out the doggy door in hot pursuit of my fantasy leaving his biscuits for me. I had to perform this little trick repeatedly before Mopp finally caught on to what was happening. She is slow. And then she got it—deception, that was deception. The next time her bigoted friend was over, Mopp explained what I had done. The friend said it sounded to him as if I was just trying to chase Hawken away from his biscuits, and that was not deception. He wanted to know if I had ever deceived HER? Mopp said she didn't think so. I had to come up with a new educational tool.

So, one day when Mopp went to work, I planned another little "deception" and spent a few hours "laying the trap." I found an old bone with just a little good stuff remaining on it and buried it in the garden. I intentionally did not do a good job of burying—I didn't put it very deep and piled up lots of dirt so it formed an obvious lump. Usually, when Mopp came home from work, she petted me, I did my greeting, took a quick pee, and immediately went down to the kitchen so she ccould make my dinner. But this day, instead of going to the kitchen, I went out the doggy door. I knew Mopp would be worried about me if I didn't go directly to my dinner bowl. I expected her to follow me outside and she did. I walked over to the old bone under the pile of dirt and sat down next to it and gazed at the lake. Mopp came over to me and stood next to me. Several times I briefly glanced at the pile with my best guilty expression. Mopp is slow but eventually she got the idea. She went to the pile and dug up the bone. At first she laughed, then she got quiet and just stared at me. Then she called her friend and told him what I did. That did it. I don't know about her friend, but Mopp was clearly convinced that I had tried to deceive her. If humans are as intelligent as they like to think they are, why did it take me so long to teach one of them something so simple and obvious?

There was an interesting post script to this deception business. A few months later, a neighbor was visiting and, as usual, their language tumors took over. They talked and talked some more. My name came up so I listened. Mopp was telling the neighbor about my getting Hawken's biscuits and hiding the bone in the garden. The neighbor was torn between staring skeptically at Mopp and staring admiringly at me. Then Mopp laughed and said that, of course, these weren't highly intelligent or complicated deceptions. I couldn't believe it. To me, that was the final test of "who is smarter, humans or coonhounds?" Mopp never did understand that I had devised these intentionally "simple" deceptions in order to demonstrate to her that I understood the concept of deception and practiced it. And, worse, she never thought of the possibility that if I were capable of highly intelligent and complicated deceptions (which I was), she would never have discovered the deceptions. And she never did. And this is for the best. If humans knew that we were smarter, they would expect us to work and provide good stuff for them. I'd rather sleep and hunt and let them work.

Willie and Stripe

I developed a few friendships of which Mopp disapproved—I guess she thought they might be a bad influence or have fleas or something. Mopp was a wildlife rehabilitator. I was all for this. She got baby raccoons, squirrels, rabbits, and birds and took care of them until they were old enough to run around the woods by themselves. What a great team we were. She got them grown up and active and I got to chase them after they were wild again.

One of her first "babies" was Willie—a tiny raccoon who had lost his mom. Mopp had the mistaken idea that, being a coonhound, I would hurt this little guy given half a chance. But she was wrong about that—Willie wasn't enough of a challenge, he actually liked me. But Mopp didn't know this and, at first, I wasn't allowed to get too close. Mopp let me watch (from a distance) while she fed Willie. At first, he drank only milk. Then, she tried to get him to eat food. But Willie wanted his milk. When Mopp tried to force him to eat the food, he spit it at her. She emerged from these feedings with great tasting stuff splattered all over her clothes. She let me lick it off her clothes before she washed them. Finally, Willie's brain engaged, and he started eating. Then he got an "outdoor" cage. One morning, before Mopp was up, Willie figured out how to get out of his cage. I was wandering around and saw what he was up to. He ran right over to me—I could hardly hurt him when he was so trusting. So we became friends and I showed him around the premises. I didn't explain the doggy door—being friends was fine but I didn't want to sleep with him. Finally Mopp woke up and found us wandering around together. At first, she got upset but then realized I wasn't going to eat him and she calmed down. She didn't show him the doggy door —guess she didn't want to sleep with him either.

With Willie

A little digression. The reason Willie was able to open his cage was because Willie had thumbs. Until I met him, I never understood what practical little things thumbs were. He could pick food up with his paws, he could open a cage door, he could move a rock and get the bugs underneath. And humans had thumbs. Those thumbs are far more important than the language tumor. Because Mopp had thumbs, she could open cans, she could open the refrigerator, she could open the dog food bag. Can you imagine of what I would have been capable if I had had thumbs? What fun I could have had!!!! What food I could have had!!!!

When Willie got a little older, Mopp left his cage door open so that he could come and go when he pleased. For about a week, he wandered around the yard and Mopp helped him learn to find food. She lifted up rocks for him so he could get bugs and took him down to the lake where he found little frogs. Weird appetite. One day when Mopp came back from work, she couldn't find Willie anywhere. She was a little upset but thought he would come home when he was ready. We didn't see him for three days, and Mopp began to worry about him. She said he was too young to be on his own. Then she looked at me in an unusual way—I could tell one of her "ideas" was coming.

Mopp got Willie's pillow from his cage, let me smell it and said, "find him." I didn't budge until she got some biscuits to take along. I get paid for the work I do. I actually wasn't sure I could tell the smell of one raccoon from another but thought I'd give it a try. So I took off down the driveway towards the forest. At one point, I smelled raccoon but didn't know if it was Willie. I left the road and walked into the forest toward the smell. Mopp was calling, "Willie, Willie." Soon there was a scrambling in the bushes and out came this dirty little raccoon. He ran over to Mopp and grabbed onto her legs. This was a bit much! Had to be Willie, what other raccoon would be so dumb. Mopp picked him up, put him on her shoulder. I felt like I was in a Disney movie. I had to nudge her biscuit pocket because she was so excited about finding Willie, she forgot to give me my reward. She gave me all the biscuits, said I was great, and we all walked home. By the time Mopp put Willie on his pillow, he was sound asleep. In the morning, she bathed him (coconut oil shampoo, poor raccoon) and gave him special treats. My reputation was made. That night I got a real bone with some meat still on it. Mopp told all her friends about my great skill in finding Willie. I was a heroine again. About a week later, Mopp took Willie away. She said he was going to go with some other raccoons his age to live in a park.

One friend of mine who Mopp did not appreciate was "Stripe." I don't know her real name. That was my name for her because she was all black with a white stripe down her back. One day I was out in the woods and "Stripe" was just there. I didn't hear or smell her; she just showed up. Sort of looked like a cat—in fact, at first I thought it was a cat. She smelled—I think "interesting" might be the kindest description but she did smell like the sort of thing to chase and definitely not the sort of thing to eat. But I couldn't chase her if she didn't run, and she just followed me and followed me, occasionally rubbing against my legs. As with the cats, I found this behavior sort of creepy. She didn't seem to want anything other than company. Eventually, I got tired of the woods and decided to go home— well, "Stripe" followed. When we got home, Mopp was outside messing in the garden and didn't pay too much attention to us. I think she thought "Stripe" was one of our cats. But then she looked more closely. "Stripe" and I went down to the lake to get a drink and Mopp just stood and stared at us like she had never seen me before. Then Mopp went inside and shook the biscuit box. Well, I couldn't ignore that so I took off to get my biscuit. Much to my surprise, after I got a few biscuits, Mopp ran over and blocked the doggy door with a chair so I couldn't get out. Usually she only did that if there was food outside she didn't want me to have. Well, no big deal, I needed a nap anyway.

But what was going on? Mopp went outside and I watched out the window. "Stripe," by this time, had gotten tired. She had short legs and the long walk probably exhausted her. She fell asleep in the flower bed. Mopp carried a plastic box and quietly and slowly walked up behind "Stripe" and quickly put the box down on top of her—trapping her inside. Then Mopp got a board and slid it underneath the box. She picked up the board, box, and "Stripe" and walked away down the driveway. About 20 minutes later she was back—no "Stripe." I guess Mopp didn't like her. Mopp came over to me and sniffed like she expected me to smell bad—I never smell bad. She seemed satisfied because I didn't get a bath. Apparently, Mopp just moved "Stripe" to the woods at the end of the driveway because, for a few months after that, I ran into "Stripe" while out hunting. She was always nice to me—cute little thing but she never did smell quite right. And she never followed me home again—I don't think Mopp made her feel welcome.

Gardening

Gardening was an activity that both Mopp and I enjoyed tremendously. Tilling up the soil in the spring, getting it all loose and easy to dig. The garden was an excellent place to bury bones, deer skins, and Mopp's smelly old shoes that she couldn't possibly want any more. Once I got into a little trouble for burying one of Mopp's shirts. She was not amused and made some nasty comment about the aesthetic sensibilities of coonhounds. But the benefits of gardening far outweighed the difficulties. The garden was a good place to dig a cool, shallow bed for a morning nap on a hot summer day.

Just enjoying life

Gardening has occasionally been a source of conflict between Mopp and me. When I was still in puppyhood, Mopp went out to the garden one afternoon. She had a shovel and a bucket filled with little hard things—sort of like the balls she used to throw and expect me to run after. I didn't understand the purpose of this—if she threw the ball and realized she had made a stupid mistake because she had meant to keep the ball, I was happy to get it for her—once! But then she threw it again and I had trouble tolerating those who can't learn from their mistakes so she just had to go get that ball herself.

These were different. Mopp didn't throw these little balls. They were some sort of treasure because she buried them just like I buried my treasures. She got down on her hands and knees and buried a few, then moved a few feet, buried a few more. Well, if there was one thing I had learned in my young life, it was that there is usually something delicious and wonderful about buried treasure. So I just followed her and dug them up. My intention was to eat them but they didn't taste very good so I just left them. That was strange because even though Mopp's food wasn't always or even usually great, it was edible and these little balls were not edible. When Mopp was done burying all the little balls and I was done unburying them all, she stood up and turned around. I suppose I couldn't really blame her for being mad. Obviously, she buried these things to keep them a secret. I don't like it when Hawken digs up my treasures. Then she laughed and started over again but watched me carefully. She didn't have to worry. The little balls weren't worth the trouble.

About a year later, Mopp came home from work and had a huge bag of blood meal with her. That bag smelled great, just great. What a perfect present for a great dog. I couldn't wait. She spread the blood meal over the garden—wonderful, wonderful. But then she put wood shavings and old leaves on top of the blood meal. WHY????? Why would she get me this present and then make it difficult for me to enjoy it? This was one of those break downs in communication. Mopp bought me this huge bag of great stuff and then mixed it up with tasteless, odorless junk. Maybe, she meant it as a challenge. Could I eat the blood meal without eating the wood and leaves? Of course, I accepted the challenge. That night, after an early and sound nap, I went out by the moonlight and, while Mopp slept, I dug through the wood shavings. I ate every bit of blood meal in the garden. What a fantastic treat. Unfortunately, I couldn't help accidentally eating some of those wood shavings. Wood shavings are not the easiest thing to digest. I had to vomit here and there and now and then for the next few days and then had diarrhea for awhile. But no big deal, it was worth it. Sort of like putting road-kill through a food processor. Mopp never bought blood meal again.

Perhaps the most controversial gardening activity involved raccoons. But first a little digression on the relationship between raccoons and coonhounds. Coonhounds are, without doubt, fantastic at tracking and treeing raccoons. This requires an exquisite sense of smell (mine was the best of the best) to find and track the raccoons and sufficient stamina to chase these little critters through the woods all night. The rules of raccoon hunting are that the coonhound or hounds pick up the scent, track the raccoon and eventually chase him/her up a tree. Key to this enterprise is the continual, ear piercing baying or howling (what Mopp calls "screaming"). Voice quality is absolutely crucial for a coonhound. Since both my folks were champs, my voice was exceptional. The howling is necessary so that the people with guns can follow us (people cannot smell but they can hear). When we have sent a raccoon up a tree and the people catch up with us, they shoot the raccoon and we (the ones who did all the work) get to eat the raccoon. Now those are the rules. And I did my bit. I picked up the scent of many raccoons and tracked them through the woods for hours and hours and hours howling and screaming the whole time so that Mopp could follow me with a gun. One night I tracked and howled and screamed for 7 hours. I was exhausted and still no Mopp with a gun. Was the woman deaf? I finally gave up and went home. She was sitting on the deck drinking wine. She hugged me, gave me a biscuit, and went to bed. A biscuit?? I deserved a raccoon. At first, I was pissed. I did my bit, where was she???? Being a lazy drunk. But then, I relented. When I thought about it more, I realized that I loved the tracking and howling. It was just plain fun even if Mopp didn't participate as she should have. And, better still, I could do it when I felt like it. When I was tired, I could sleep with no expectations that I would work all night long. Then raccoons came to the garden, and everything changed.

One nice spring day, Mopp put dozens and dozens of little plants in the garden. She was smiling and obviously pleased with her work—at least until the next morning. Unfortunately, most of the little plants had been dug up and strewn around during the night. At first she thought I might have done it. How unfair. I was asleep all night, and I have better things to do than dig up stupid, inedible plants. I knew that raccoons had done the damage. I could smell them. But I could only understand language, I couldn't speak it so Mopp would have to figure this out for herself. Mopp put all the plants back in their proper place in the garden. The same thing happened that night—they were all dug up and thrown around. The next day, Mopp planted them all again but, this time, she sprinkled some white powder around the plants. The next morning, most of the plants were dug up again. Mopp examined the white powder and looked at a book, then said, "raccoons." Very clever. Mopp couldn't smell the raccoons but she could see where their feet had been in the white powder and these were raccoon prints. Humans aren't always stupid.

Mopp now knew raccoons were responsible for coming into the garden at night and digging up all these little plants. I was wondering about the intelligence of the raccoons—why did they do this?? Was this a little game to play with Mopp? Was this their idea of fun? Mopp, with her ever-crazy logic, blamed me. She said, as she put the plants back into the garden every morning, "aren't you a coonhound? Why don't you chase these guys away?" Well, the answer was simple, I was sleeping. She didn't wonder why there were no raccoons digging up plants during the day—she didn't give me credit for guarding her silly little plants during the day. I can't be awake all the time. I did not have a ready answer for her next question: "How can you hear a cat vomiting and yet not hear raccoons ripping the garden apart?" I pretended I didn't understand English. But I could just tell that there was trouble ahead—Mopp started talking to herself. Ever since the "ice cube in the doggy door" solution, Mopp thought she could creatively solve life's little problems. Sometimes she created worse problems than she was trying to solve. But what can you expect from humans. Me—I'd just forget the plants. What good were they anyway.

Her first plan was to put one of my beds on the deck near the garden. She was hoping that I would choose to sleep outside and wake up when the raccoons visited and chase them away. No go. I did take naps outside sometimes but the frogs and crickets were so noisy and, with the cats running around, it was impossible to sleep. Besides, Mopp's bed was far more comfortable than any of my beds. She threatened to put me outside and block the doggy door so that I would have to sleep outside but I knew she wouldn't do that—it was not a nice way to treat her coonhound companion. I was right, she didn't. Plan #2: Mopp purchased this little device that made a horrible and loud sound when something moved in front of it. She put this thing in the garden. The "plan" was that, when the raccoons came, they would set off the alarm system, the alarm system would wake me up, and I would dash outside and "do my duty," as she put it. Unfortunately for the plants, when the alarm went off, Mopp woke up but I didn't. I sleep rather soundly because I work hard when I'm awake. Furthermore, this dumb little device didn't just go off when a raccoon passed by but also when I passed by to take a midnight pee. Scared me to death. I was not happy, Mopp was not happy. She put those little plants back in the ground again.

Plan #3 involved the additional purchase of a small tent. The plan was that Mopp and I would sleep outside in this tent-thing so that when the alarm went off, I would be close enough to hear it. I would then wake up, and "do my duty." If I didn't wake up, Mopp would wake me up. The first problem was the cats. The tent was too small so when Mopp or I moved, we pushed against the side and the side bulged and moved. The cats thought this was a game—everytime Mopp or I moved against the side, the cats attacked from the outside. We had to lie very very still which, of course, was impossible when you know that there is a cat crouching out there waiting to pounce the second you move. Mosquitoes were the second problem. Mopp wanted to keep the flap of the tent zippered shut to keep out the mosquitoes, but I thought a zippered tent a bit claustrophobic and hot. This was not fun, we were not getting any sleep and the raccoons were probably sitting up in some tree laughing at us. I decided this whole plan was silly. I went back inside, went upstairs away from all this confusion, and went to sleep in Mopp's bed. Then it started to drizzle, then it started to really rain. Soon Mopp came back in. She was wet and had a truly bad attitude. She gave me a dirty look, and went to sleep in her bed where she should have been in the first place.

We didn't try camping again. The next morning, she put those plants back in the ground again.

Mopp found Plan #4 in a book. This required soaking rags in ammonia and spreading the rags around the garden. It worked for a few days (it certainly kept me out of the garden). But then I guess the coons decided they didn't mind the smell or the ammonia dried because they came back to cause more trouble. Plan #5, suggested by a friend, was to scatter human hair all over the garden. I didn't hear the logic behind this one—why would a raccoon stay away from hair? But we were desperate or, rather, Mopp was desperate. The person who cuts her hair collected hair for her and gave her several huge bags of the stuff. Mopp spread a thick layer of this throughout the garden. Not only did the hair not keep the raccoons away but it looked kind of creepy especially when it was wet. Plan #6 was to liberally sprinkle chile powder all over the garden. The morning after she tried that, I came outside to find her putting those plants back in the ground and talking to herself. She was planning a money making scheme—she was going to sell human hair sprinkled with chile powder as raccoon treats.

I found it difficult to sympathize. What's the big deal? The raccoons weren't stealing food. Fortunately, Mopp gave up her campaign against the raccoons. She put more little plants in the ground so that the raccoons could have some and she could have some. And we returned to our normal sleeping routine.

The Rabbit in the Bucket

Coonhounds are actually somewhat handicapped in the pursuit of "live" outdoor dinner. The minute I smelled potential food, I got so excited, I started to howl and scream. This made it impossible to sneak up on a critter and grab dinner. That is, by the way, why humans with guns are supposed to accompany the coonhounds. Since Mopp didn't do her bit, I was left on my own. And I had trouble keeping my mouth shut. Hawken, however, was not a screamer and quite good at stealth. At times, we were able to work well together. However, one of our uniquely unsuccessful attempts occurred one night when Hawken was sleeping over.

We went to sleep early—about 10. We wanted to be rested for later—we had hunting plans. Around 2 AM, we went out and down to the lake for a drink. We sniffed the air and tried to decide where to go, what to do, what kind of trouble we could find. Then I noticed Thoby, the orange cat, crouched near some bushes and being very, very still. Thoby was not the brightest of the lot but I was nice to him because he never finished his food and I got what was left. Given his IQ, I usually didn't give him much notice but then something moved in the bushes. Suddenly, a rabbit shot out of the bushes heading toward the lake with Thoby right behind him and Hawken after Thoby and me after Hawken. The row boat was turned over with the back end lying in the water. The rabbit ran up the boat and just flew off the end right into the lake with Thoby right behind him and Hawken right behind Thoby. I hate to get wet, so I watched from shore while all these folks went swimming.

What happened in the lake remains a mystery. Soon Thoby came out followed by Hawken with the rabbit in his mouth; I was impressed. All of them were dripping wet. We all went back to the house and through the doggy door. I tried to explain to Hawken that if he took the rabbit inside, Mopp would take it away from him. But he was too cold (being all wet) to stay outside so we all went in trying to be very, very quiet. Not only did Hawken go inside, he went upstairs and got on the couch with the rabbit. No way this was going to work out well.

I tried to tell Hawken that Mopp would wake up and we would all be in big trouble. We weren't allowed to bring dead animals in the house, and we certainly were not allowed to get on the couch after swimming. But he wouldn't listen to me. He probably thought I was trying to get his rabbit (and I was). He had just settled down on the couch when we heard unusual noises coming from Mopp's bed. Thoby, who was dripping wet, had jumped on top of Mopp. Mopp woke up and reached to pet him and screamed. She thought the "wetness" was blood and that Thoby was injured. I could just tell this was going to be a long, long night. Mopp turned on the light, realized Thoby was just wet with water, and stopped screaming. Unfortunately, she decided to get up to check on us. She walked into the living room and turned on a light. The first thing she saw was Hawken on the couch, dripping wet, with a small, wet animal in his mouth. She looked at me like somehow this was all my fault. She probably thought the rabbit was dead and I had killed it. If she hadn't been so tired, she would have realized that if I had killed a rabbit, I would never have given it away. I tried very hard to look innocent. With exaggerated calmness, she told us to "stay," repeated this three times, and went downstairs. If I had had the rabbit in MY mouth, I would have been out the doggy door in a flash but Hawken has this "obedience" problem.

Mopp came back upstairs with her standard issue "getting rid of disgusting stuff" equipment—bucket, rags, rubber gloves. She started walking toward Hawken when suddenly the rabbit moved. Hawken had not killed it. What was he waiting for? Mopp stopped dead in her tracks. She clearly didn't know what to do. She started talking to herself—always a bad sign. She said, "There is a live muskrat on my couch—how do I handle this?" Muskrat?? Then I understood. Mopp thought it was a muskrat because it was wet, and she thought muskrats were dangerous. (I caught one once and it bit through my lip; the trials of being a coonhound.) She looked at me again. I tried to feign sleep but she wasn't fooled. She just would not believe that I was not responsible for this particular mess. I guess I understood why, and I had pulled many capers and tricks for which I never got blamed. Payback time? But, no. That is the sort of logic stupid people use when they bet on "heads" after a run of "tails."

Back to the story. Mopp thought Hawken had a live muskrat hanging from his mouth. She walked towards Hawken very, very slowly. She carried the bucket upside down in both hands. When she was standing immediately in front of Hawken, she said suddenly and very loudly "drop it." She was obviously counting on Hawken's being an obedient dog—which he, unfortunately, was. He dropped it and Mopp, acting quicker than I thought her capable, slammed the bucket down trapping her "muskrat" inside. She grabbed some books and piled them on top of the bucket to weigh it down so that the critter couldn't tip it over and escape. She went downstairs and got a piece of plywood. This she slid under the bucket trapping the critter. She carried the whole mess—plywood, critter, bucket—downstairs and outside very, very carefully. For some unknown reason, she grabbed a rake and flashlight on the way out. Hawken and I, even Thoby, followed close behind. This was going to be interesting. Maybe rabbit dinner was still a possibility.

Mopp walked down to the lake shore, took a big breath, and threw the whole mess into the lake—she thought the "muskrat" would feel "at home" in the lake. She grabbed the flashlight and the rake, planning to retrieve the bucket and plywood. She shined the flashlight towards the lake. The bucket was upright and the "muskrat," having dried a bit, was clearly a rabbit and was sitting in the bucket. The bucket was floating away from shore. All hell broke loose. Once Mopp realized the "muskrat" was a rabbit, she worried that it might not know how to swim and would drown. She tried to bring the bucket back to shore with the rake but it had drifted out too far. She grabbed the rake and the flashlight, ran to the boat, turned it over, and hopped in. This night was becoming tediously long. Although I had not had adequate sleep or food for all of this action, I didn't want to miss anything. So I leapt into the boat. Who knows, maybe rabbit dinner was still possible. Mopp rowed and rowed and rowed and used the flashlight to search the whole lake and the shore. I got so bored after an hour or so that I asked to be taken to shore. Mopp let me out of the boat near the house. She went on with her search while I went inside and joined Hawken in some much needed sleep. To this day, neither the rabbit nor the bucket has ever been found. And I had to go to sleep hungry.

California and Condoms

I had wonderful friends. I had people friends, dog friends, cat friends (well, sort of), and "other." My people friends were mostly Mopp's people friends. Humans seem to vary greatly in their ability, or maybe their desire, to communicate. Most of Mopp's friends had the ability and the desire to communicate with me, and these were my friends. Mopp implied that I didn't give people much choice—they could hardly ignore my unusually charming but loud voice, nor could they miss that their food disappeared when they weren't looking. But just because humans might be annoyed with me or notice me does not mean that they can actually communicate with me. The losers might say to Mopp, "Make your dog stop eating my food." Or, "tell your dog to be quiet." Really, "your dog?" I don't belong to anyone and my name is Emma and they should talk to ME, not to MOPP. Oh well, just one of my human peeves. But these folks clearly didn't "fit" and rarely were invited back a second time unless Mopp thought they had potential.

Perhaps, the ability to communicate well with dogs is inherited. I met Mopp's mom and sister. Mopp wanted me to meet her mother, and her mother couldn't travel so we had to go there, and it was a long way. So when I was about 6 months old, we took an airplane to California. I find it difficult to describe the airplane. First, we went to a huge building with many, many people. Mopp made me get into a big cage—I could tell she didn't want to do this which some how made it all worse. She said she would see me in a little while. And then someone carried the cage with me in it to a dark, strange place. There were no other humans or dogs. I think there might have been a cat somewhere but the place was dark, and there were many bad smells and much unpleasant noise. I was hungry and thirsty and lonely. I did not like this mode of travel. Eventually, the noise stopped and someone carried me still in my cage, and there was Mopp. She was excited and happy to see me. She started crying and gave me water and food and took me outside to pee. Mopp's sister, Vicki, was there also. She looked and smelled like Mopp—how interesting. And she was one of those people who "got" dogs. She petted me and talked to me and gave me treats and thought I was beautiful.

Then Vicki drove us to Mopp's mom's house. What a nice, nice friend she turned out to be. She also looked like Mopp and smelled like Mopp. This could get confusing. Mopp's mom couldn't walk and zipped around in a chair with wheels on it. Mopp said she was my gramma—not sure what that meant but at least I had name for her. Mopp told me that her mom had always had dog companions until she became unable to walk. Gramma's house did not have woods and a lake—just a tiny little yard with a fence—not much fun. But every morning Mopp drove us down to the beach for our jog. WOW! What an interesting place that was. I got to run in the water and chase the birds. There was lots to eat—old hot dogs, bread, sausage. There were many other dogs at the beach and I made some new friends. Mopp often stopped to talk to the human companions of the dogs, and they all asked her what kind of dog I was. Apparently, coonhounds did not live in California and some people didn't even know what a coonhound was. There were raccoons in California, I could smell them but not at the beach and that was the only place I could run around without a leash. I couldn't show my stuff.

Gramma liked my company. She always invited me to hop up on her bed when she took a nap. And she talked to me because she knew I could understand her. She saved me bits of her dinner and asked Mopp to buy some special treats for me. There was a noticeable lack of items to chew on so I chewed up Gramma's hair bursh one sunny morning. She thought it was funny. Great lady. One day, Mopp drove Gramma and me to visit Vicki's house. She had children and cats but I was not allowed to chase the cats. The children were nice. They always seemed to have food with them which they shared with me. Well, they didn't have much choice. They were so short, I just helped myself. I've met children before and they are not all nice. Some like to pull on my ears and stick their fingers in my eyes and grab my tail. But Vicki's children just petted and shared their food. Mopp said they were my cousins whatever that is.

Chewing up Gramma's brush

We stayed at Gramma's about a week. I had a good time but I was ready to go home and back to the woods and raccoons and Hawken. Vicki drove us to the airplane. Not this again. The cage, the noise, the horrible smells. Scary and lonely. After a long time, my cage was carried off the airplane and put on a moving sidewalk. I thought it was about time to express my displeasure with this mode of travel. I just howled and howled and howled some more, as loud as I could. I had had enough of this. My trip on the moving sidewalk contraption took awhile, and I just kept howling. Eventually, my cage moved into a big room and there was Mopp and many other people just standing there staring at me as my cage moved closer and closer. The howling sounded great in this big room, lots of echoes. Mopp grabbed the cage and opened the door so I could get out. She hugged and kissed me and told me I had a wonderful voice. She said I had provided great entertainment for all these people, and they were impressed with my wonderful voice. They didn't look impressed, just rather amazed. That was my last airplane. I do not like airplanes.

While we were in California, I overheard a conversation that Mopp had with Vicki. Mopp told her that I had hurt my foot a few months earlier but that I insisted on jogging with her in spite of limping. Vicki said that Mopp should make me stay home if I had a limp ("make me???"). Mopp replied that she assumed I knew best—if it bothered me too much I wouldn't go. Vicki said, "You don't know when you are too sick or too injured to go jogging, why do you expect Emma to know what is good for her?" Well, that shut Mopp up. But Vicki was right. You would not believe the conditions under which we went jogging: pouring rain, thunder and lightening storms, ice storms, 16 inches of snow, and -50 degrees wind chill factor. One had to seriously question Mopp's sanity when she went jogging with a cracked rib, the flu, bronchitis, surgery the previous afternoon, 2 hours sleep—this woman was nuts. I always complained a bit about "bad jogging conditions" just to get sympathy and extra treats but I actually enjoyed it—certainly better than sitting around indoors doing nothing and waiting for the next season. Mopp did take pity on me and bought me a winter coat—made in England, cotton shell with flannel lining, extra large. It was wonderful but embarrassing. However, the times I needed this thing, there were no other insane persons or animals outside to see me.

My injured foot reminds me of another embarrassment Mopp forced on me. I had a thorn embedded in my foot and kept getting infections. Finally, not with my consent, I had an operation. I had to miss dinner and spend the night in a cage before surgery. Not a good experience, and I was not quiet about my displeasure. My voice, lovely and appropriate in the woods, was apparently a bit too much for the vet hospital. My doctor told Mopp I had whipped up the other dogs into a howling frenzy. So what was wrong with that? It did relieve the boredom a bit and the other dogs seemed to have fun. Anyway, Mopp came the next day and picked me up. The doctor told her I couldn't get my heavily bandaged foot wet for a week.

Mopp muttered to herself all the way home—how I can keep a dog with a doggy door from getting her foot wet when there is a lake next to the house and rainy weather? She tried plastic baggies but they tore easily. She ripped up an old raincoat and made a boot but it kept falling off. A few days after the operation, she came home singing and talking to herself with a smug look on her face (one of her schemes). She took out this little package and (you won't believe this) put a condom on my foot. She told me what a condom was (yuck—people are so weird) but said that this was the only way to keep my foot dry. She tried to persuade me by saying it had ribbing on it so I could get traction with the foot. What truly persuaded me, however, was when she told me that if I got my bandage wet, I would have to go back to the doctor. The condom actually wasn't a bad solution. Dogs and raccoons didn't know what a condom was so they didn't make fun of me.

One Whole Dead Deer

I do apologize for returning again and again to food but food was of major importance in my life. If only there was some way to enjoy my woodland treats without bad consequences. The inevitable sequel to enjoying some tasty morsel from the great outdoors was, what Mopp called, "your disgusting farts." She then knew I had a secret stash, and it usually wasn't long before she managed to find my snacks and throw them into the lake. I had a superb, superb, superb sense of smell, and I didn't think this very natural process was disgusting. My olfactory ability was 1,463,734 times better than Mopp's. So who are you going to believe—Mopp or me?? Mopp burps all the time, I don't complain about the noise. Burps remind me of one of the times I regretted my decision not to learn to speak English. A man came to our house to fix something in the bathroom. While he was working upstairs, Mopp was downstairs reading and eating her breakfast. When she was done, she let out this loud, long, truly disgusting burp. Then she got a horrible look on her face. Obviously, she had forgotten this man was upstairs. Then she saw me, smiled, and said, (more loudly than necessary) "Emma, that's disgusting." I couldn't believe it. I was a scapegoat. If there had been a way I could blame her for the farts, I would have, believe me. And the more embarrassing for her the better.

Back to my food quest! On one beautiful, sunny but cool day, I was out in the woods looking for entertainment and found the biggest and best prize. A whole dead deer, not too far from the house. My first thought was that this could keep me happy for months. My second thought was that I had to be very, very careful not to let on to Mopp about this prize. The deer was lying on the other side of the lake right next to the water. When Mopp left for whatever it is she does, I strolled over for brunch, then lunch, then mid-afternoon snack. After a few days of wonderful indulgence, Mopp noticed my extended belly and commented on my "disgusting farts." She knew immediately what I had found and what I was eating. I could tell from her expression that this was "not OK" even though I followed the rules—I didn't bring it inside. The next morning when she was busy, I thought it would be safe to get a snack. Little did I know, she was spying on me and, unfortunately, discovered the location of my treasure.

Mopp got the boat out and rowed over to the deer. I just sat there and watched, wondering what she would do. She tried to pull the deer into the lake with an oar. I couldn't believe it—she was going to throw the whole thing into the lake. I ran around the lake to the other side where the deer was. As Mopp tried to pull the deer into the lake, I tried to pull it back out with my teeth. This tug of war went on for awhile. Eventually, she won but only because she had a head start—I got there too late. She started to pull away from the shore, pushing the deer in front of the boat with an oar. NO WAY. I took a flying leap and landed in the boat. I tried to lean over the side to grab the deer while Mopp tried to keep pushing it further out in the water. Unfortunately, we were both leaning on the same side of the boat, and we were leaning too far—we both fell into the water as the boat went up on its side. Mopp was not happy, neither was I. We both swam to shore, Mopp pulling the rope attached to the boat with her. The deer continued floating out toward the middle of the lake. Mopp mumbled some not-too-nice words as she pulled the boat in. Soggy and cold and unhappy, we both got into the boat and Mopp rowed us back home. At least she didn't make me walk home. I vowed that this was only a temporary defeat.

I wasn't about to go swimming after the deer so, for three days, I sat on the shore and watched and waited. Occasionally, I took a walk around the lake to watch the progress of the floating deer. Finally, it came to rest on the shore again—a different side of the lake but readily accessible, and I happily began my feasting again. I did this while Mopp was at work or in the middle of the night so Mopp wouldn't know that the deer had drifted into shore again. Unfortunately, the consequences of feasting again became obvious. Everytime I passed a bit of gas, Mopp looked at me suspiciously. The more I feasted, the more she sniffed and complained. One day she came home earlier than usual and found me at it. Trouble. I could tell she was thinking and thinking, trying to come up with one of her "creative" solutions. After another day, she opened the refrigerator and removed about 10 jars of hot sauce. Every summer, uncle Blair and uncle George visited and they always brought a jar of some new hot sauce they had discovered. But Mopp didn't like the stuff so the jars accumulated. Hot sauce smells bad and tastes worse. Mopp emptied all the jars in a bowl and mixed them together. Then she added about a cup of cayenne pepper and a little vinegar and mixed again. With a self-satisfied smile on her face, she took this horrible mixture into the boat, rowed over to the deer and poured it all over my dinner. Well, that did it. I truly tried to eat it but it was awful and I had to drink so much water, I could barely move. I returned everyday for five days—still not appetizing. But then it rained, washing away all the hot sauce, and the deer was mine again. I resumed feasting.

A few days later, Mopp invited Kelly and Jerry for dinner. Of course, the invitation included their three dogs—my friends—Hawken, Necco, and Sampson. As the three people were sitting down to eat, I decided to have my own dinner party. It was not part of my nature to share great treats BUT I knew it was only a matter of time before Mopp realized the deer was edible again, and I was tiring of this game. So the four of us strolled over to the remains and finished it off—a great, great party. When we returned a few hours later, our people were just finishing their dinner and happy to see us until Necco threw up. Fortunately, we did not get into too much trouble. They were focused on the cats. Apparently, one of the cats had left a partially eaten dead frog under the dining table and one of them stepped on it with bare feet.

The wonderful deer was gone but my "disgusting farts" continued to cause trouble. One December day we were invited over to Jill's and Lana's for Christmas dinner. Great. Food—vegetarian food but food nonetheless. Christmas comes at the tail end of hunting season so there had been good treats in the woods. And I had indulged a bit earlier in the day. I was not feeling so good but could always enjoy more food. So off we went to dinner. At the time, Jill and Lana had two dogs—Muffy who was a tiny, tiny little dog and Maggie who was almost normal size. The first thing I did whenever we visited these folks was to find and devour the chew hooves and raw hides these silly dogs leave lying around unattended. That done, I took a nap in anticipation of a good dinner.

Dinner smelled great. I figured the best place was under the table. This was a tight squeeze with all the feet under there but I managed and laid down waiting for the people to drink a bit too much wine and start dropping food here and there. But then my stomach started up—that pleasant, gurgling feeling, a build up of pressure and the slow release. Too much dead deer. After awhile, I realized that everyone was sniffing and peering at me under the table. Mopp suggested I go elsewhere to sleep. I refused. She insisted. I reluctantly obeyed and got up on the couch where I could watch. Everyone kept sniffing and staring at me, saying things like "overwhelming" and "oh, that was a bad one." After a few more minutes of this, Mopp, with a resigned look on her face, got up from the table and called to me. She was laughing but then said it was time to go home. Home? People were still eating, I hadn't even licked plates yet. Mopp said "good bye." We got into the car and I sulked. Then Mopp explained that she wanted me all to herself on Christmas. Well, that was nice, very nice as long as she had remembered to shop for groceries. Mopp put my window down so I could get my head out. Surprisingly, she also put her own window down even though it was incredibly cold outside. She turned the heat on "high." My idea of a great Christmas and I hadn't even gotten my presents yet.

A Day in the Life of a Coonhound

Over the years, Mopp learned well the lessons I taught her. She became the perfect coonhound companion. Of course, I had to learn a few things from her and became the perfect human companion. Fortunately, we enjoyed a similar life style—fun, good food, and comforts. Mopp was big on comfort—both hers and mine. In the winter, Mopp made a fire in the wood stove and put one of my beds near it. I also had a heated bed that plugged into the wall but this was really designed for a dog smaller than me, and I preferred to be near the wood burner. Or I could snooze on the futon which had a mattress warmer but that was a favorite nap place for cats; I dislike sharing with cats. Maybe I'm allergic to them. In the summer, Mopp put one of my beds out on the deck so I could nap outside while she messed around in the garden. Or, my favorite nap spot of all time but practical only in warm weather—Mopp opened the door of the car so that I could sleep on the back seat. Nice breeze, able to keep an eye on all outdoors but still a bit of protection—even in the rain. All in all, I can't complain about the nap options. Unless someone in the woods needed my attention, I slept until Mopp had breakfast. She ate vegetables, of all things, for breakfast. I got a few biscuits. After breakfast,

I did "rounds." I checked the house perimeter, garden, car, and lake and did the digging, chewing, and chasing that was needed. If I felt energetic or if Hawken was visiting, I'd take a walk around the lake. All this could take a few minutes or a few hours. Regardless, I never neglected my duties—well, except when there was a thunder storm or it was very cold.

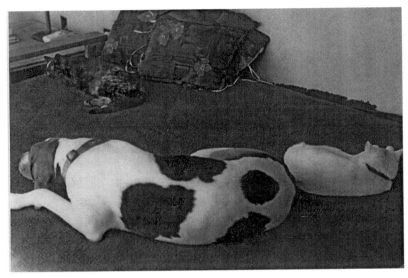

Sleeping with Clem and Hester

Sometimes Mopp left for the day, sometimes she stayed home but, for me, afternoon was coma time. I needed this time to rest and recuperate. I could not tolerate noises or disturbances in the afternoon. If Mopp was home, she was appropriately quiet. She usually read or wrote. I trained the cats to be quiet. Occasionally, a man would be there who made noise all day long. He had saws, drills, hammers—every noise maker you could imagine including the radio. Unbearable. But, under normal circumstances, I slept undisturbed. If Mopp went to "work," she was usually back around 5. On these days, I woke up at 4:59, stretched, and managed to get outside and act like I had been waiting patiently and guarding the house all afternoon just as she drove down the hill.

Then we went for a nice, long walk into the woods or around the lake. We both loved this late afternoon walk—slow, pleasant, relaxed, unless I found something to track. If I did, Mopp knew I could find my way home, so she let me do what I wanted. Sometimes one or more of the cats accompanied us. They slowed us down a bit. I never could understand why cats can't simply walk along in a straight line. They have to crouch, pounce (on nothing), take off into the bushes, run up trees. All of these behaviors make perfect sense if they were actually pouncing on something or chasing something but they seemed to just have an active fantasy life. Thoby occasionally got tired and complained until Mopp picked him up and carried him on her shoulder. On days Mopp stayed home, we usually would drive somewhere to go for a walk. Sometimes we met people friends—sometimes they had dog friends with them. One of my favorite walks was Campus Lake. I liked walking near a lake because I could get a drink when I needed one. Or take a swim if it was hot.

The best part of this lake was the food. The lake was loaded with ducks and people brought bread to feed the ducks. Well, it was certainly no problem to chase a few ducks away and eat the bread. Sometimes people gave the bread to me directly rather than going through the intermediary steps. I got bigger pieces that way but Mopp yelled at me if she saw me asking for bread. There was a student cafeteria along our route. Great, great smells. There were always people standing around outside eating. I tried, rather unsuccessfully, to look like a hungry stray. Mopp thought that was rather funny—she said it would take quite a disguise for me to look like I was not well fed. But these folks hadn't yet learned not to litter so there was always food on the ground. French fries, parts of sandwiches, chicken pieces, sausage. Once I found most of a hamburger with lots of mustard on it. My face was yellow for several days. Usually Mopp tried to spot the food before I did and throw it into a trash can but I'm faster than she is and have a far superior nose so I could smell the food before she could see it. I also figured out how to get food out of the trash cans but it left a mess and Mopp said I would get arrested if someone saw me do that. Arrested??? She said "arrested" was like staying overnight at the vet but without a comfortable bed and without good food. No thanks. Occasionally, I found a dead fish lying on the grass. This was not particularly appealing as food but great for a good roll. I got that great smell all over my body, even between my toes and in my ears. You can imagine what Mopp thought about this. I, of course, got a bath after listening to Mopp complain all the way home in the car—with all the windows open.

My favorite time of day was dinner time. I always got the same old dry stuff which was good but boring. Mopp, however, realized this and always put something interesting and particularly tasty on top. My favorite was chicken livers. I was grateful that she didn't expect ME to be a vegetarian. And I got to lick the cat bowls when they were done. After dinner, I slept for an hour or so until Mopp's dinner time. When Mopp ate, I got biscuits. She let me lick her plate but she was very stingy about what she left. Sometimes it didn't seem enough to make it worthwhile to get off my bed. Then I really slept, slept soundly so that I'd be ready around midnight to go out exploring a bit. Usually, I found nothing worth much effort and went back home to sleep. Occasionally, especially in the fall, I found a scent interesting enough to track. And track I did with my beautiful and strong voice. I was off for hours doing what I was born to do—the best feeling in the world. Eventually, after a few hours, I returned home exhausted, hungry, and happy. Mopp was always up and awake, waiting for me. She never scolded me for my mid-night activities. I know she would rather sleep than listen to my howling but she understood—she loved me and she loved my voice. She gave me a few biscuits and a hug and then sent me to bed. I slept like a puppy.

Note to the reader: Because I did not waste my brain and my time messing around with language, I have had to rely on Mopp for translating. This has caused me some concern. Communication systems vary greatly on the dimensions of precision and subtlety: when I saw a pile of raccoon poop, my description included the time lapsed since it was deposited, the direction the raccoon was headed, the age of the raccoon, the sex of the raccoon, and what the raccoon had for dinner. This rich description was translated by Mopp as "a little pile of raccoon poop." I'm sure you see the problem. The second concern was, of course, that she may not have translated accurately 'cause it might make her look bad. So, any part of my story in which I was not portrayed as beautiful, intelligent, sophisticated, charming, flexible, adorable, clever, and a champion coonhound must be suspected of bias in the translation.

Epilogue

Sleeping in the Forest

I thought the earth
remembered me, she
took me back so tenderly, arranging
her dark skirts, her pockets
full of lichens and seeds. I slept
as never before, a stone
on the riverbed, nothing
between me and the white fire of the stars
but my thoughts, and they floated
light as moths among the branches
of the perfect trees. All night
I heard the small kingdoms breathing
around me, the insects, and the birds
who do their work in the darkness. All night
I rose and fell, as if in water, grappling
with a luminous doom. By morning
I had vanished at least a dozen times
into something better.

Mary Oliver

About the Author

Emma died from heart failure in 2000. Linda Gannon was a psychology professor at Southern Illinois University from 1975 until her retirement in 2006. Although she has published books and articles in her professional discipline, this is her first book written for a general audience. Dr. Gannon currently lives in rural southern Illinois with Willow the Weimaraner, Thoby the orange cat, Oliver the gray cat and many wild lives.

LaVergne, TN USA
24 February 2011
217760LV00001B/151/P